WHEN WE DON'T understand...

WHEN WE DON'T
understand...

God's ways with Jonah and Habakkuk

John D. Legg

 EVANGELICAL PRESS

EVANGELICAL PRESS
12 Wooler Street, Darlington, Co. Durham, DL1 1RQ, England

© Evangelical Press 1992
First published 1992

British Library Cataloguing in Publication Data available

ISBN 0-85234-291-8

Printed in Great Britain at the Bath Press, Avon.

Contents

I. Introduction

1.
Problems and the Bible

A friend once told me that he never had any problems with believing the Bible in general, or believing in the existence of God in particular, until he read a book (by the great Charles Hodge, of all people), which tried to answer the problems! It is to be hoped that this present work will not come under the same condemnation. Bearing this cautionary tale in mind, I am nevertheless encouraged to proceed by two considerations.

The first is that many people do have problems. Some, like Habakkuk, can and do put their difficulties into words; others, like Jonah, simply react against God, without trying to sort things out. These are the problems with which pastors must grapple and with which individual Christians must try to cope, sometimes without help.

The second encouragement is that these particular problems are not men of straw, set up for the purpose of being knocked down. They are to be found in the experience of real people in the Bible, together with the answers. Further, they are still to be found in the experience of Christians, who need those same biblical answers.

It is at this point that God's wisdom becomes very apparent in the way he caused the Bible to be written, containing not only doctrine, commands and history, but also experience — the accounts of people with difficulties, which had to be and were resolved — concrete examples, practical illustrations.

'You can't believe everything you read in the Bible'

'Heresy!' you exclaim and rightly, too, in the sense in which these words are usually meant. But let us think about this a little further. For instance, take the words found in Psalm 14:1: 'There is no God.' Is that true? Are the devil's words in Genesis 3:4-5, 'You will not surely die', true? Of course not! Yet they are Scripture, parts of verses, chapters, or books, which convey the truth of God. The truth of the whole contradicts the untruth of the parts, which are accurately recorded words of unbelievers, or even of Satan. Similarly, Job, Jeremiah and various psalms contain words and expressions where the author is fighting his way through doubts and fears to a place of safety and certainty.

We must be careful not to stop reading too soon, for on the way the biblical subject will express himself in ways which seem, and often are at the time, unbelieving or almost blasphemous. The combined effect, though, of the whole psalm or book is true. In God's wisdom, men are allowed to express their doubts and perplexities, their fears and even their disagreements and quarrels with the Lord, so that they may be dealt with thoroughly and we, in our turn, may be helped.

The whole of the Bible is God's Word; it is all infallible, but we must be clear in what sense this is so. It is true that the fool says that there is no God; it is true that the devil lies; it is true that men doubt and worry, and that their faith falters. It is also true that God works in them to keep them and, by his Spirit, enlighten them, or, as in Job's case, to preserve them in the faith even where they do not understand. It is this larger message which is true and, moreover, immensely valuable to us.

It is often difficult to discern what the truth is which we are to believe and apply, but it is by no means impossible. The practical must be understood in the light of the doctrinal; the doctrinal must be seen worked out in experience. We have to learn to distinguish between ways in which truth is expressed. It is quite wrong to treat Paul's letters in the way I have just described; it is absolutely necessary to adopt this approach with Jonah and Habakkuk.

People, not just problems

Just as we interpret one verse in the light of the whole psalm and Zophar's words in the context of the whole book of Job, so we must understand Jonah and Habakkuk progressively, as God deals in stages with the situation in which the prophet is found at the opening of the book. Indeed, there may be as much to learn from the way in which the Lord deals with the individual as from the actual answers that are given. These books are not dealing merely with theoretical or philosophical problems, although these are very prominent. Here we have actual people, whose attitudes and actions have to be changed. Jonah must go and preach to Nineveh; Habakkuk must respond positively in the midst of an invasion. They are just as real and just as needy as the troubled soul who consults his minister, the perplexed student who is reading this book or the backsliding friend you are trying to help.

It is this practical aim that is our real safeguard. We shall not be sitting back in our armchairs, discussing God, or even our problems about God. We are all involved; we cannot afford to be arrogant before God, or superior towards Jonah or Habakkuk. This book is, technically, a 'theodicy', an attempt to justify the thoughts and ways of God to man, apologetics for the believer on, I hope, a sound biblical basis and in a biblical manner. But we shall avoid intellectualism and sterility only if we realize that we have to do with practical issues which demand a response — with real, indeed common, experiences, and ones which may be ours.

Although Jonah appears to begin with a simple case of disobedience to God's command, it soon becomes clear that more is involved and before we have finished we are concerned with the whole issue of God's justice and love. Habakkuk seems to move in the reverse direction. We start with a theological difficulty: the problem of evil. Then, it becomes evident that much more is involved and we finish by confronting the whole question of the sovereignty of God in personal, national and church life.

These problems are present at all times. The form they take may and will vary, but you and I do face these same issues — if not every day, at least very often. There is a Jonah in all of us in our relationships with the enemies of God. There is a Habakkuk in all of us as we face the desperate situation of the church today. We need to know, not just how to answer the questions, but above all how to respond ourselves to the situations that confront us. Our consideration of Jonah and Habakkuk should help us to do just that.

II. Jonah and the love of God

2.
A representative Israelite

The first thing to establish is the relevance to us of Jonah and his problems, the link between an Old Testament Jew and twentieth-century Christians. To do this we must look at Jonah himself.

Scholarly research has produced few assured results about the origin and author of the book of Jonah. It may have been written by the prophet himself or it may not. It may have been written after the exile, but no one is certain. About Jonah himself, however, we need have no doubt.

Jonah the prophet

Jonah was a real prophet, living around 780 B.C. In 2 Kings 14:25 we read that King Jeroboam II of the northern kingdom of Israel 'restored the boundaries of Israel from Lebo Hamath to the Sea of the Arabah, in accordance with the word of the Lord, the God of Israel, spoken through his servant Jonah son of Amittai, the prophet from Gath Hepher'.

It is important to stress this, because many, perhaps in an attempt to avoid the miraculous elements in the story, treat the book of Jonah as fiction. Thus a Jewish propagandist is said to have invented the story to make a universalist point, i.e. against Jewish exclusivism, at some point in the later history of Israel. Alternatively, to give a more spiritual tone to the same approach, the book is said to be a parable, forgetting that parables, as distinct from allegories, are real-life stories. According to one 'evangelical' scholar the author deliberately linked his non-hero with the prophet of 2 Kings, whom he regards as 'a nationalistic prophet', ideally suited to be 'the butt for an attack on religious nationalism'. In the real world of Christian principles, this scholarly device would be called libel, no less immoral because the man libelled is dead. This is not to deny that the book has a clear point, only to reject the notion that the facts which are used to make the point are fictitious.

It is quite clear that Jesus himself regarded Jonah as a real person, as real as the men of his own day or the Queen of Sheba. He gave a solemn warning in Matthew 12:41-42: 'The men of Nineveh will stand up at the judgement with this generation and condemn it; for they repented at the preaching of Jonah, and now one greater than Jonah is here.' His words would have had little force if his hearers could have retorted, 'But that's only a story!' It is equally important for us to insist that it is not just a story: that Jonah was a real prophet, that the events recorded in the book really happened and that we, too, are to take note of them.

Furthermore, Jonah was a true prophet. It is vital for the lesson of the book to recognize this. The whole issue of Jonah's disobedience and repentance depends on his being a true prophet — one who actually received a message from God, whose declaration of judgement was an infallible statement of the purpose of the Lord. This is clearly why he refused to go. If he went, he had no choice, but to say what God had told him to say, with all the inevitable and unwelcome consequences which he foresaw. He could not, and would not, alter the message in any way. The only alternative was not to go to Nineveh at all. The message was as true as the one delivered to Jeroboam II, which proved accurate.

It is important to distinguish between the inspiration of the prophet's words and the quality of his life. The words of the prophets, in both the Old and the New Testaments, were infallible, the very oracles of God, expressed by the words, 'This is what the Lord says,' or 'what the Holy Spirit says'. Generally, of course, their lives were godly and obedient, but they were not perfect and the authority of their words did not rest upon the quality of their lives. They spoke from God, but they were still sinners and very fallible in practice. Thus the prophets and apostles spoke, as it were, *ex cathedra*, but their actions frequently left much to be desired. So Peter was rightly rebuked by Paul for his sin at Antioch (Galatians 2:11-14), but that did not contradict his apostolic authority in teaching the Word of God. Paul, also, was a sinner, but his words were the Word of God. Jonah was disobedient, but a true prophet all the same.

However, Jonah was an unusual prophet and the book is an unusual prophetic book, in that there is hardly any prophecy in it! The whole message of Jonah, delivered to Nineveh, consists of the words found in chapter 3:4: 'Forty more days and Nineveh will be overturned,' and even these words had no direct relevance to the Jewish readers. This also marks out Jonah in another way. As far as we can tell, no other prophet actually delivered his messages of judgement against the heathen *to* the people concerned. Such messages in Isaiah and other prophets were basically intended for home consumption and the foreign nations were not expected to know of them or do anything about them. So it is not Jonah's *message* that is important for the Jewish readers or for us; it is the prophet's *history* that is significant; the man is the message. It is God's dealings with his disobedient servant that provide the teaching for the Israelite readers.

We are, therefore, forced to the conclusion that Jonah appears in this book as a representative of the ordinary Israelite rather than as a prophet. (He is not actually called a prophet in the book, though this is not unique to Jonah.) His calling is their calling; his message is their message; his disobedience is their disobedience. God's dealings with Jonah indicate what they ought to be and do. As they read about Jonah they must reflect on their own attitudes and ways — and repent.

And so must we. We are not at liberty to sit in judgement on this narrow and disobedient prophet. We, too, are under scrutiny and subject to the judgement of God. We today are not exempt from this penetrating, often devastating, exposure of the frailties, follies and sins of the people of God. As the Jewish reader followed the story of Jonah, he was brought face to face with his own responsibility. If we are to follow this for ourselves, then we must be clear just what Jonah was called to do and why he went in the opposite direction.

The church's prophetic calling

There is much wrong talk about prophets today, but the aspect of this which is valid is generally overlooked, namely, that of the corporate prophetic calling of the people of God. We are accustomed to thinking of Christians as priests and kings in Christ. Old Testament priests and kings were not only types of the coming Priest-King, the Lord Jesus Christ, but also representatives of all the Israelites, who were called to be 'a kingdom of priests' (Exodus 19:6). What is less often recognized is that the prophets, who were 'servants of God' in a special sense, as well as foreshadowing the great Prophet mentioned in Deuteronomy 18, represented the whole nation's calling to be 'the servant of the Lord'.

Israel was called to be God's messenger to the heathen nations. This was symbolized by the lights in the sanctuary, whether the seven-branched lampstand in the tabernacle or the later temple lamps. It was because they did not fulfil this calling that *the* Servant of the Lord, Jesus Christ, was appointed to be 'a light for the Gentiles' (Isaiah 42:6). In verses 18 and 19 of that same chapter, the Lord exclaims,

> 'Hear, you deaf;
>   look, you blind, and see!
> Who is blind but my servant,
>   and deaf like the messenger I send?
> Who is blind like the one committed to me,
>   blind like the servant of the Lord?'

Following this condemnation of Israel, in chapter 49:6 we read these words, addressed to the Messiah, who will do what they have failed to do:

> 'It is too small a thing for you to be my servant
>   to restore the tribes of Jacob
> and bring back those of Israel I have kept.
>   I will also make you a light for the Gentiles,
> that you may bring my salvation to the ends of the earth.'

This is not to say that Israel should have engaged in missionary work — to Nineveh or anywhere else — in those days; they were times of preparation. Nevertheless, the nation should, at least, have shown forth the character and glory of God. The temple should have been a demonstration of the way of salvation through sacrifice and have been seen as a 'house of prayer for all nations' (Isaiah 56:7). The prophecies of future blessing for the Gentiles should have kept them from the kind of narrow exclusivism that is condemned in Jonah.

If, then, these blessings and promises should have kept Israel of old from such an attitude, how much more ought we to have an awareness of our prophetic calling as the Israel of God! If we are to be 'a kingdom and priests' (Revelation 1:6) and 'a royal priesthood' (1 Peter 2:9), then we must also see our calling to be the servants of God to declare his message, to make known the excellencies of the One who called us out of darkness into his marvellous light. This is not just for preachers; in particular, it does not refer to what is commonly regarded as 'prophetic preaching', i.e. denouncing the evils of the day in strong language. Still less does it refer to self-styled, contemporary, individual prophets. It is the universal prophethood of the church, which was predicted in Joel 2:28-32 and which began to be fulfilled on the Day of Pentecost:

'In the last days, God says,
  I will pour out my Spirit on all people.
Your sons and daughters will prophesy...'

(Acts 2:17).

Whatever else Revelation 11 may have to teach us, it surely draws our attention to this same fact. The two witnesses in verse 3, symbolizing the church, are said to 'prophesy'. They are described as olive-trees and lampstands, recalling both the vision of Zechariah 4 and the churches of Revelation 1-3, and then represented as latter-day prophets, with powers resembling those of Moses and Elijah.

If we want to read Jonah properly we must put ourselves in his shoes. The Word of the Lord came to Jonah, son of Amittai. The Word of the Lord has come to us. We have his gospel; we have his Spirit. We are called to be his servants, to bring light to the Gentiles of our day. What are we doing about it? Are we behaving like Jonah? (Hold your answer to this for a while!)

Next we must see the situation in which this calling is to be exercised. No longer is Jonah to minister to Israel, not even to the wayward and idolatrous northern kingdom. He is to go to Nineveh and prophesy in an ungodly, heathen world. The description of Nineveh recalls the Lord's sentence on Sodom and Gomorrah: 'The outcry against Sodom and Gomorrah is so great and their sin so grievous that I will go down and see if what they have done is as bad as the outcry that has reached me' (Genesis 18:20-21). Jonah was called, Israel was called, and we are called, to exercise a prophetic ministry of denunciation against the great city of the world.

This we must do, then, not in the sense of advancing political solutions to current national problems, but declaring the Word of God. And this we must do, as Jonah did, in Nineveh, not from the safety of a suburban pulpit or the security of a rural study, but where people are. It was one thing for the prophets to thunder their denunciations of Edom, Moab, Assyria and Egypt to a sympathetic audience in Jerusalem, to assure the people of God of the Lord's defence of them and his victory over his and their enemies. It was another for Jonah to go to Nineveh and challenge its wickedness face to face. Although there is no suggestion that it was this consideration that made Jonah refuse to go, it is something that we must bear in mind. God calls the prophetic church to testify to the judgement of God where sin abounds. We must not be afraid to go among sinners and declare God's message. Prophetic ministry — whether by ministers or 'laymen' — does not consist of cosy messages delivered among friends, but of declarations about sin and wrath made in the front line, where we live or work, where sin abounds and saints are few — a ministry often best performed by those who are not full-time preachers.

The church must be obedient to this calling. Previous obedience and reputation count for nothing; like the boxer, we are only as good as our last fight! Jonah, who had spoken boldly to Jeroboam, disobeyed and fell. Not only did he not go to Nineveh; he went off in the opposite direction. The text asserts that he tried 'to flee from the presence of the Lord'. It would be foolish to interpret this as a crude denial of the omnipresence of God in defiance of Psalm 139:7-8:

> 'Where can I go from your Spirit?
> Where can I flee from your presence?
> If I go up to the heavens you are there;
>   if I make my bed in the depths, you are there.'

As Jonah was to prove, and as he must surely have known anyway, you do not get away from God by leaving the land of promise, as if the Lord were one of the Canaanite gods with his own limited territory. According to verse 9, Jonah knew that the Lord is 'the God of heaven, who made the sea and the land', not some minor territorial deity.

What, then, is the point? A reference to the ministry of Elijah, who is constantly brought to mind in the course of this book, will help. In 1 Kings 17:1 Elijah announces himself as one who serves the Lord, 'before whom I stand' (NKJV). A prophet was called into the throne-room of his King to receive his instructions as he stood before the Lord. This Jonah has done, but he refuses the task; he will not work as God's servant. He has, as it were, resigned his commission in God's army, a situation which recurs in chapter 4, when he says he would rather die than go on serving such a God.

So he leaves the presence of God, inevitably forfeiting his favour and blessing. In the same way, Christ's assurance of his presence with his servants, 'Surely I am with you always, to the very end of the age', depends on obedience to the preceding command: 'Go and make disciples of all nations' (Matthew 28:19-20). You and I have been called, not as individual prophets, or necessarily as preachers, but as the Israel of God, to witness against our modern Nineveh, to declare God's wrath and judgement, and if we desire to keep the blessing of God and to enjoy his presence with us, we must obey.

Like Jonah, we may have problems of various kinds — with ourselves, with our enemies, with the difficulties of the situation. We may not understand, but we must obey. If, like Jonah, we even disagree with the Lord, then we must seek his face and search his Word by the aid of the Holy Spirit, until we submit and agree. Then we can go ahead with our prophetic calling, not unwillingly, but wholeheartedly. The last thing we should do is despair because we have failed the Lord once, or even many times. Remember Jonah! You are not unique in your failure. You are not alone in your perplexity. And like Jonah you may find an answer.

3.
Jonah's error

In the prophecy we are not told until chapter 4 why Jonah disobeyed, and then only indirectly. However, it will be helpful for us to look at Jonah's reasons at this stage, so that we may see more clearly the wisdom of God in his dealings with him throughout the book. In any case we should not assume that the Jewish reader was similarly 'in the dark'. No doubt he understood Jonah's attitude perfectly — for the very good reason that he agreed with it!

This is the whole point of the book. While we are, at least initially, appalled at Jonah's action, the Jewish reader would be completely in sympathy with him. He may have been perplexed, because it involved disagreeing with the Lord, but this was true for Jonah himself. He simply could not understand how the Lord could tell him to do such a thing. Indeed, he was angry with God — and the original readers could share in this too.

This, however, is no reason for us to feel superior. It will, I trust, become clear as we proceed that, in spite of our apparent commitment to evangelism and missions, we are more like Jonah than we would care to admit publicly — and that without any of Jonah's excuse. Jonah's problem was with the love of God, with God's attitude to the Ninevites, his enemies. The same problem afflicts the church in general and individual Christians today. So let us ask why Jonah behaved as he did.

In chapter 4:2, after the Lord has had compassion on Nineveh, Jonah shows his displeasure and complains to the Lord. It is called a prayer, perhaps because he asks the Lord to take away his life, but is, in fact simply an angry remonstrance: 'O Lord, is this not what

I said when I was still at home? That is why I was so quick to flee to Tarshish. I knew that you are a gracious and compassionate God, slow to anger and abounding in love, a God who relents from sending calamity.' Quite obviously, he objects to the fact that God has spared Nineveh; he has 'relented from sending calamity'. Why?

Some answers

Various suggestions have been made, some of them rather subtle — over-subtle it seems to me — because the authors cannot really believe that Jonah was as bad as he appears.

It is proposed that Jonah was concerned for his reputation as a prophet. He was afraid that he would prophesy the downfall of Nineveh, but then the Lord would let them off, making a mockery of his words. Previously, what he had prophesied had come true (see 2 Kings 14:25), but now he would be made to look ridiculous in the eyes of the Ninevites and even of his own countrymen.

Such a view betrays a very low view of Jonah's intelligence. Jonah knew very well, as did the Ninevites and the other Jews, and as we should, that prophecies of this kind are always conditional. The possibility of repentance removing the threat was implied even when not stated. The Ninevites' repentance was based on this supposition and so was Jonah's anger. They and he would accept that his prophecy had been successful; it had produced the desired effect — desired, that is, by God, not by Jonah!

Unlike many modern readers, Jonah had no difficulty with the idea of God 'relenting' (or 'repenting', as older versions have it), as if God had somehow been diverted from his original purpose. There is no contradiction between Jonah 3:9 and 4:2, which speak of him relenting or repenting, and 1 Samuel 15:11, 29 and 35, which say that he does not relent like a man. The latter verses assert that God is not fickle like a mere man. He does not have to change his mind because he has made a mistake or an error of judgement. He does not have to relent because of the force of circumstances, because he cannot put his threat into practice. He always does what he has purposed, fulfils his promises, carries out his threats in accordance with his character. Malachi 3:6 sums this up perfectly: 'I the Lord do not change. So you, O descendants of Jacob, are not destroyed.' Jonah's complaint is based on this. He knew what God is like. He could refer to Exodus 34:6-7 and say, 'I knew that you are a gracious God...'

No, God's purpose does not change; nor does his character. What, then, does it mean when the Bible says that he relented or repented? In the first place, it means that God in his purpose has ordered not only the ends but also the means. He had always designed that the Ninevites should be saved; he had also ordained that this would come to pass through the preaching of Jonah. This is what I meant by saying just now that his prophecy of judgement had the desired effect.

Secondly, prophecy was given in certain circumstances; impenitent Ninevites were threatened with judgement and if they had remained in their impenitence, there is no doubt that the judgement would have descended upon them. However, if the situation changes, if the reason for the prophecy is no longer there, then God's declared attitude alters accordingly; wrath turns into mercy, judgement into blessing, in accordance with God's character. The people have changed, the situation has changed, but God has not changed. He, in his constancy and unchanging faithfulness to himself, has adopted the attitude and taken the action appropriate to the new situation.

A second, even more subtle, reason which has been suggested, is that Jonah was concerned for the good of his own people, Israel. This takes two forms. Either, it is claimed, Jonah was worried that if the Ninevites were spared, they would continue as the foes of Israel and in time destroy them, or he was concerned that the Ninevites should be punished as an example to Israel, who had departed from the Lord. There is nothing, however, in the text of the book to support these suggestions and they seem to me to presuppose too high a view of Jonah. There is no hint that Jonah was bothered about anything other than himself and his own ideas.

God's fault!

The real reason is very simple. Jonah was angry because he thought it was God's responsibility and duty to punish the great and wicked city of Nineveh. They deserved it and, if God is a just God, he should have done it. He knew God would not, and could not, punish them if they repented, but thought he was wrong to allow them this possibility. So Jonah was angry. His attitude in 4:2 is quite clearly, 'I told you so.' He knew that God would forgive them if they repented, but thought God was wrong to be merciful to these wicked heathen by giving them the opportunity to repent. He is still justifying his previous disobedience; he has, as it were, been trying to save God from himself!

In reality God had not dealt with the Ninevites as Jonah had hoped and as any Jew would have expected. He wanted them punished. They were sinners — great sinners. They worshipped heathen gods; they defied Jehovah and oppressed his people. So Jonah was disappointed because God could have shown his justice and really dealt with these enemies of the true religion once for all, but he had failed to do so. This is confirmed by the Lord's challenging question in chapter 4:11: 'Should I not be concerned about that great city?' It is perfectly clear that the issue is simply whether God should care about the Ninevites or not. The answer of Jonah and, we may be sure, of the average Jewish reader at this time would have been a resounding 'No'.

Now it may reasonably be asked why Jonah, who in 4:2 could quote God's gracious promises from Exodus 34:6-7, 'I knew that you are a gracious and compassionate God, slow to anger and abounding in love, a God who relents from sending calamity,' should now deny this. The answer is, of course, that for Jonah these promises in particular, and God's grace and mercy in general, were for Israel, the covenant people. The heathen Ninevites were outside the covenant of promise and excluded from all the benefits of God's grace. They were beyond the pale — outsiders and opponents to be punished by God's justice, so that Israel could be safe to enjoy all the covenant blessings of God's mercy.

Now, to rejoice in God's covenant mercy and grace was correct as far as it went — gloriously correct — but Jonah, like others before and after him, had clearly misunderstood the nature of Israel's election and calling. They were God's people and he was their God, but that was not the end of the story. Israel, as we have seen already, was to be God's servant to spread the light to the whole world; through Abraham and his offspring all nations were to be blessed (Genesis 12:3; 22:18). Salvation was both for the Jews and, through the Jews, for others (see John 4:22-23). All this Jonah seems to have rejected or ignored.

His idea was to take pride in Israel's calling, as if they in some way deserved it. Pride naturally and inevitably leads to despising others; despising leads to hating them, and hating leads to taking pleasure in their punishment, downfall and death. (God, on the contrary, declares that he takes no pleasure in the death of the wicked, Ezekiel 18:23,32.) At the root of Jonah's wrong attitude, then, is a failure to see that Israel's position was entirely of God's free grace. They had neither merit nor anything else that could cause God to choose them. He had done so out of free, unmerited and sovereign grace, as Deuteronomy 7:6-8 makes clear: 'For you are a people holy to the Lord your God. The Lord your God has chosen you out of all the peoples on the face of the earth to be his people, his treasured possession. The Lord did not set his affection on you and choose you because you were more numerous than other peoples, for you were the fewest of all peoples. But it was because the Lord loved you...'

For us too, a correct attitude to unbelievers, to enemies of the gospel, must begin with this same realization. Contrary to popular opinion, a belief in the sovereign grace of God, far from inhibiting evangelism, is the only true and liberating basis for a genuine concern for the lost of all nations. Some refuse to acknowledge that God has chosen and saved us in sovereign grace, not because we are good, or many, or potentially useful, or for any other reason in us. He saves, he makes useful, and we can have no pride at all if we see this. Then we see that we are not free to despise anybody, far less hate them or delight in their suffering. As Paul reminds Titus in chapter 3:3-5, 'At one time we too were foolish, disobedient, deceived and enslaved by all kinds of passions and pleasures. We lived in malice and envy, being hated and hating one another. But when the kindness and love of God our Saviour appeared, he saved us, not because of righteous things we had done, but because of his mercy.' This is the only proper basis for a right attitude to others who are, as yet, outside the sphere of God's mercy, i.e. to the modern equivalent of the Ninevites.

Our practice

Now, how does this work out in practice? We can see how it worked out for Jonah; the enemies must be destroyed, not saved. So it was, too, for the Jews of the author's time and for many centuries before and after. There are many implied references to Elijah in Jonah and he had a similar attitude. In 1 Kings 19 he virtually demands that God revenge him upon the apostate Israelites and, especially, on Jezebel and Ahab. As Paul puts it, 'He appealed to God against Israel' (Romans 11:2). God's reply was heard, not in the wind, earthquake or fire of judgement, but in the still, small voice of mercy.

The Pharisees adopted the same attitude. Jesus portrayed them as the elder brother in the parable of the prodigal son. *He* was the chosen one; why should this rebel receive grace? He ought to be punished (Luke 15:25-31). The disciples followed Elijah's lead in 2 Kings 1 (although on that occasion Elijah, in his context, was right) by offering 'to call fire down from heaven to destroy' the Samaritan villagers who had dared to refuse hospitality to Christ on his way to Jerusalem. Remnants of the same rejection of Gentiles linger on even in the Acts of the Apostles. Enemies, whether outright heathen or apostate covenant-breakers, should be punished, not shown mercy.

This has continued down the centuries. Enmity between nations has blinded Christian men to the need of sinners and persecution has ensued instead of evangelization. Anti-Semitism regarded it as a pious duty to kill the murderers of Christ. The earnest and sincere, as well as the grasping and cruel, went on crusades to annihilate the Muslims who had 'intruded' into the Holy Land. But surely, you may argue, we today do not approve of these things? We feel the shame of the crusades and of the many anti-Jewish pogroms, do we not?

The fact is that we are all Jonahs, even today. Sometimes it appears in a modified form, when we preach the gospel to people in a condescending way, but refuse to accept them as equals in the church: whites and blacks, lower classes and upper classes, the drug-addicts and misfits. Beyond this, however, we find the actual attitude persisting. Even today, after years of the gospel message, after years of reading Jonah, after years of seeing the example of Christ, Christians — real ones, even those most eager for conversions — hold back when it comes to those whom we regard as our enemies, or even just as God's enemies.

It is said that the gospel has not been preached properly in the Muslim north of Nigeria, because these people are regarded by those in the south as foreigners and enemies. Similarly it is true that we do not bother about our hereditary enemies, whether it be a neighbouring tribe, a different class or the branch of the family with whom there has been a long-standing quarrel. When the old China Inland Mission was forced out of China and began to look for an alternative mission field, it was only with the greatest hesitation that Japan was seen as a possibility. To their great and eternal credit they did decide, under their new name of the Overseas Missionary Fellowship (OMF), to take the good news of mercy and forgiveness to those who a few years earlier had oppressed their beloved Chinese brethren and attacked the Western nations to which most of them belonged. There are still many who have great reservations, not always put into words, about evangelism to, and forgiveness for, Germans. Can the Nazis really be saved? Can we bring ourselves to wish, hope and pray that they will escape their well-deserved judgement at the hand of God?

Coming even nearer home and to the present day, we find many Christians who will pray for poor deluded Roman Catholics, but find the priests and, above all, the pope, utterly beyond the pale. They are only objects of (holy!) hatred — to be denounced vociferously, not prayed for, or witnessed to. (The editor of a Christian magazine was denounced roundly for daring to postulate the possibility of the pope's conversion!) We worry over those who get involved with the Jehovah's Witnesses and try to protect them or rescue them from being led astray, but the couple at the door, accompanied by children and armed with copies of *The Watchtower*, are enemies of the faith and of ourselves, to be attacked and seen off as quickly as possible, rather than lost souls to be wept over.

Child-molesters, IRA terrorists or UVF assassins we see only as people to be dealt with by justice. Those who offend us or attack the gospel are sinners to be opposed, the enemies of God upon whom we call down fire from heaven. Muslims, vandals, the rich and powerful racketeers, the pornographers, the drug-pushers — you name them — all who oppose God, as distinct from merely going on their sinful way without bothering us — we rejoice if they fall foul of the law, if the IRA bomber blows himself up, or the drug-pusher dies of AIDS. After all, it just serves them right. To God be the glory, the modern Nineveh has been punished, and quite right too! The idea that they should be saved and forgiven and received into the fold of God hardly crosses our minds. Justice is everything.

How easy it is to become hard! A concern for justice need not

be arrogant or hypocritical, but it is difficult to avoid this consequence. When the justice of this world ignores or justifies the most
awful sins and even crimes, a tender Christian conscience will
object and long for real justice. When foolish theories are put
forward, in contradiction of the plain historical facts, to deny that the
Jews were responsible for the crucifixion of Christ, we resist it as
folly, if nothing worse. (God did, in fact, judge them in A.D. 70, just
as God did judge Nineveh and Babylon eventually.) We object when
perversions are legalized and sins are excused or blamed onto
society in general. All this is valid, but how often this is taken a stage
further and, feeling superior because we do not do these things
ourselves, we act as judges and deny the gospel to such people! (It
is surely this sentence of death which contravenes Christ's words in
Matthew 7:1-2 about not judging, rather than mere assessment.)

Anti-Semitism may be a consequence of taking the Bible
seriously, but it is still the wrong consequence. Modern Jews are still
hounded as 'Christ-killers', as we read in Stan Telchin's book
Betrayed! Probably, we personally do not do this, but it is a similar
attitude which judges those who oppose that same Christ today.

Can we afford to look down on Jonah? Examine yourself to see
who and how many you have excluded from your compassion,
omitted from your prayers and deprived of your testimony. And ask
why. Is it because they are too bad, because they do not deserve
God's mercy? Have they, in your estimation, put themselves beyond
the pale? Then the Lord must deal with us as he dealt with Jonah.

4.
God deals with the prophet

Before the Lord puts Jonah's doctrine and theology right, he puts *him* right. The root of Jonah's problem is not in his head, but in his heart. This is not to say that the doctrine is unimportant. Far from it. However, we must realize that before Jonah can learn the doctrinal lesson, he must learn the spiritual one, and the same is true of us all. There is a necessary work of preparation which God alone can perform, before we are ready to heed his correction of our theology. Our whole attitude to God and to his salvation must be transformed before our particular problem can be dealt with. Our attitude to ourselves must be altered before our attitude to the undeserving ungodly can be changed.

Because of his wrong ideas — his conviction that, really, God was in the wrong — the disobedient prophet tried to run away from the Lord, but discovered that this was something neither he nor anyone else can do. We have seen already that Jonah did not have a crude ignorance of the omnipresence of God. In fact, he was resigning his commission. Jonah was no longer prepared to obey God, so he left the scene of his service and went in the opposite direction from that of his instructions. The Lord, however, did not let him go, just like that.

It may be that Jonah really thought he could get away from God. Surely, he was in the right; his guidance was confirmed by the 'open door' before him — a ship bound for his destination of Tarshish, just waiting for him! He must be doing the right thing, so he could sleep (1:5) the sleep, if not of the just, at least of a man with a clear and untroubled conscience — in reality, a dulled conscience. If we have fallen into the sinful attitude described in the last chapter, we may very well be simply going about our daily business, thinking all is well with our souls — backsliders, in fact, but not in our own eyes. Are you asleep on the job of making the gospel known, of fulfilling your calling in the world, asleep and at peace when you should be obeying? Do not think yourself 'not guilty', simply because your conscience does not trouble you. It may be that God has to deal with you as he did with Jonah.

God chastises him

The Lord begins by virtually chasing Jonah! He simply will not let him go. He goes after the backslider, just as Francis Thompson describes 'the Hound of Heaven' pursuing him 'down the nights and down the days ... down the arches of the years ... down the labyrinthine ways' of his own mind. God does not merely follow; he takes hold. He does not remind Jonah gently; that would clearly have been of little use. Instead he casts him into the sea. Although the hands were the sailors', the action was the Lord's:

> 'You hurled me into the deep,
>   into the very heart of the seas,
>   and the currents swirled about me;
> all your waves and breakers swept over me'

(2:3).

Thank God that he does this! In his sovereign grace the Lord does not leave the prophet in his sin. Nor does he wait for Jonah to return of his own accord, as some would have us believe. To many, God is helpless, waiting on the sidelines for us to yield our lives to him, waiting for us to surrender, ready to help but powerless to intervene. The truth is far different, as Jonah was to discover, and as we may take for our comfort. Even our sin and folly cannot destroy us, thanks to the grace of God. He will pursue us and bring us back.

The immediate consequences of God's unfailing love were not very comfortable — 'a great wind' and 'a violent storm' (1:4) — but all was intended for Jonah's good. What a consolation that, when we are perplexed, even sinning and backsliding, we are never out of God's hands! This is not, of course, a licence to 'go on sinning, so that grace may increase' (Romans 6:1). That is the mark of the false professor, the non-genuine Christian. However, those who truly belong to the Lord may take this comfort and believe the words of Romans 8:28: 'And we know that in all things God works for the good of those who love him, who have been called according to his purpose,' and of Hebrews 12:10-11: 'God disciplines us for our good, that we may share in his holiness. No discipline seems pleasant at the time, but painful. Later on, however, it produces a harvest of righteousness and peace for those who have been trained by it.'

Once he has been woken up, Jonah realizes that it is the Lord who has sent this storm; he is the cause of the sailors' trouble. 'It is my fault that this great storm has come upon you,' he tells the sailors. The process of correction has begun; Jonah now recognizes that the Lord is angry with him, even though, as yet, he does not admit his fault. This humbling is the first stage in our recall to right paths. If we truly belong to the Lord, then we are not content with being out of his favour. So, in the belly of the great fish, Jonah begins to think about his ways.

God convinces him of his sovereignty

As a result of the storm and the danger to the ship, Jonah recognizes God's sovereignty over all things in his providence. No doubt he believed this in theory already, but a great part of God's dealings with Jonah consists in convincing him in practice of what he knows only theoretically. The author of Jonah emphasizes this lordship of God over all things — that he 'works out everything in conformity with the purpose of his will' (Ephesians 1:11) — in various connections. It is the Lord who rules 'nature'; *he* sent the great wind (1:4). It is also clear that the Lord controlled even the casting of lots (1:7), so that it accurately fell upon Jonah. (See Proverbs 16:33, 'The lot is cast into the lap, but its every decision is from the Lord.' This, incidentally, is true even when the lot does not provide true guidance; it is still in the Lord's hands.) Even more significant in the realm of God's spiritual dealings with the recalcitrant prophet is the repeated occurrence of the word 'provided'. 'The Lord provided a great fish to swallow Jonah,' (1:17) links with the later provision, in chapter 4:6-8, of the vine, the worm and the sun. All creatures, great and small, are under his control — from worms to Jonah, and from fish to heathen sailors. 'The Lord provides' includes the unpleasant, as well as the things we usually term 'providential'!

The necessary prelude to changing Jonah's ideas about the heathen is to convince him that God is truly sovereign, a realization which carries with it the awareness that we must submit to this Lord who rules all things. Both the heathen and we, ourselves, are in God's hands. He decides what happens to us and we must adapt our ideas to his, and not vice versa. Right ideas about evangelism and missionary work begin with the acknowledgement of the absolute sovereignty of God over his creation and his creatures to whom we must make known the gospel. It is God's work among his creatures, so it must be done in his way.

God convicts him of his sin

There is no way back into God's favour apart from conviction of sin and repentance, which we find confirmed here. Already, in chapter 1:12, Jonah sees that God is displeased with him and that his fate is the work of God's justice. Although he does not see that his ideas are wrong, at least he seems to acknowledge that he has done wrong in running away from God and his service (1:10). It may be, too, that the heathen sailors have put him to shame with their efforts to avoid throwing him overboard. Has he begun to realize that they are men like himself? Is he ashamed of the contrast between their strenuous efforts to save him (1:13) and his callous leaving of the Ninevites to their fate? We Christians, even today, are too often put to shame by the 'good' heathen around us: their kindness, compassion, loyalty and friendship.

The next step in the argument of the book Jonah, presumably, did not see for himself, but the Jewish readers are confronted with the disturbing fact that Gentile sailors, heathen like the Ninevites, can be saved. This is undoubtedly the conclusion that we are intended to draw from the sailors' response in verse 16. As a result of their throwing Jonah into the sea, the storm quietened down and this clearly convinced them that Jonah's God, who had reacted in this way, was the true God and they 'feared' him, 'offered a sacrifice' and 'made vows to him' — all expressions of true religion in Old Testament terms which they would recognize.

Thus the Gentiles are converted, while the Jew is still under God's wrath and displeasure. This is all topsy-turvy! Not only can such people be saved, but those of the Jews who disobey God can be lost. Years later the Lord Jesus Christ warned the unbelieving Jews of his day, that the Ninevites, and the Queen of Sheba, would rise up against them in the Day of Judgement (Luke 11:29-32; see also Matthew 8:11-12). It may be that converted Catholics and Jehovah's Witnesses, once enemies and opponents of our gospel, will rise up against us, if we do not repent, believe and spread the gospel.

God convinces him of his need of grace

To return to Jonah, clearly he now admits his fault in disobeying and running away from his duty, although it is less clear that he agrees that it was his duty! Now it is time for him to experience God's grace for himself, as he turns back to God — a conversion in the same sense as Peter's return from backsliding referred to in Luke 22:32. The account of his prayer in chapter 2 refers back to his calling upon the Lord while in the sea, before the fish swallowed him and thus saved him from drowning. His prayer was for deliverance from death, from God's judgement on him, not for deliverance from the fish's belly. The different elements in this conversion are vital to the process of showing Jonah his error. It is only as we see ourselves truly, as utterly dependent on the grace of God, that we can view others correctly. The root of Jonah's problem was not false teaching, but pride in his own righteousness, his position as a Jew, one of God's chosen race, and until this was dealt with there was no way he could change his attitude to the enemies of Israel.

The different elements in this process are important. First, he had to be humbled. In chapter 2:6-7 he tells us how he came to an end of himself as he thought he was finished. His 'life was ebbing away' and the proud, rebellious prophet realized that he could do nothing at all to save himself. Here is the clue to many of our problems with the ways of God: we are proud. Indeed, how else could we take issue with the Lord himself and disagree with his decisions and methods? Whether, as with Jonah, it is God's love for our enemies that causes us to stumble, or more generally, God's providential dealings with us, the trouble is not in our understanding, nor in our exegesis of the Scriptures, but in our hearts.

Jonah was humbled. He saw his poverty and weakness. Later he will have to learn it again, more thoroughly, but already God is showing him that he is just as sinful, just as helpless, as the heathen he despises and hates. He has to be saved by God's grace, just as they do. In the depths of the sea, he cannot rely on his goodness or his privileges as an Israelite. He can only beseech God to help:

'In my distress I called to the Lord,
    and he answered me.
From the depths of the grave I called for help,
    and you listened to my cry'

(2:2).

With Peter many years later, he has to be able to say, 'We believe it is through the grace of our Lord Jesus that we are saved, just as they are' (Acts 15:11). He sees as never before that 'Salvation comes from the Lord' (2:9). He does not yet see the implications of this, but he is really admitting that he has no more right to be saved than anyone else — i.e. no right at all. Who is he, then, to object to the salvation of anybody, or to deny them the opportunity to repent?

So the first great requirement for fulfilling our calling to preach repentance to the world is to see that our own salvation is 'from the Lord', that it is by sovereign grace. A true experience of the grace of God cannot be inward-looking and selfish; it must partake of the attitude our Lord expected of his disciples: 'Freely you have received, freely give' (Matthew 10:8). Forget the idea, so sadly prevalent in some circles where the doctrines of grace are popular, that your own election is all that need concern you. Get rid of your pride in your ability to save yourself and you will begin to look differently on others.

Although we must not read too much into Jonah's words in this prayer in the fish's belly, it does seem that the prophet has made even more progress. He is at least beginning to change his attitude to the heathen. In verse 8 he envisages the possibility of idol-worshippers receiving grace. He declares, 'Those who cling to worthless idols forfeit the grace that could be theirs.' The word for grace is *hesed*, the special covenant word, which Jonah would really only apply to Jews! He even seems to grieve that these heathen are missing out on this. What a change!

Now Jonah has repented of his disobedience, the Lord shows his sovereignty once more and commands the fish to vomit Jonah onto the dry land, so that he can resume his work. In effect he is recommissioned. He now sees his duty to preach as a steward of God's truth, saying exactly what he is told to say: 'Go to the great city of Nineveh and proclaim to it the message I give you' (3:2). He braves the possible enmity of a great and wicked city and declares its imminent overthrow. He even implies the possibility of repentance, leading to a withdrawal of God's threatened judgement, for these enemies of God and of Israel. Why else are the Ninevites given forty days' notice of the overturning of their city, but to allow time for repentance? (2 Peter 3:9).

And yet Jonah has not changed enough. Although he now fulfils his vows (2:9) and preaches to the Gentiles, his attitude still falls far short of what it ought to be. He still has no compassion; he is 'greatly displeased' and even 'angry', because God has had compassion on the Ninevites and spared them. Here again we must take warning. Even when the Lord has disciplined us and brought us back to himself and to the way of obedience, even when we have been humbled and learned of our own need of grace, it is still possible to do the work of the gospel, to evangelize and be God's witnesses in the world, and to do it in entirely the wrong way.

We bear testimony to the gospel, perhaps even to people we dislike or are at enmity with, because we see it as our duty, and no more. Now this is good as far as it goes. God has commanded us to make disciples of *all* nations, so all nations it is. We grit our teeth and tell all kinds of people of God's judgement and mercy. Contrary to many people's ideas, it is a good motive to do something out of mere duty, for we are doing what our God wants, what will please him, no matter what our own feelings in the matter may be. But it is still not good enough. Our feelings ought to be correct. We should also have compassion as a motive — these various motives are not mutually exclusive. We may do the work for God's glory (or so we think), or because it is our calling — as minister, missionary, church member, etc., but the absence of compassion, so this story tells us, ruins our service.

In a twisted sort of way Jonah was concerned for God's honour, because he felt that God was letting himself down by forgetting to be just. This forgiving of the Ninevites, Jonah sees as a failing. In fact, it is God's true character which is his glory — his love and compassion and mercy — and it is this to which Jonah objected. God still had a lot of work to do on Jonah.

5.
God deals with the problem

In a superficial way — just looking at the narrative — chapter 3:10 is the climax of the book. Jonah has preached, the Ninevites have repented and the city has been saved. Great! But that is not the point of the book. What about Jonah's attitude of mind and heart? What about the Jewish readers who, no doubt, had agreed with his desire for the Ninevites' destruction and sympathized with the prophet in his disobedience? What about us in the twentieth century?

So far Jonah has been chastened and shown that he cannot disobey God with impunity; he has learned that salvation is from the Lord — even for him, a devout Jew — and that he, too, is dependent on God's grace; he has seen that he must follow his calling to be a light and a witness to the Gentiles, however ungodly and guilty they may be. So he has, rather unwillingly, taken up his task of preaching to Nineveh. Nevertheless, he still wants the Ninevites punished and sulks because they have escaped. He is 'greatly displeased' and 'angry' (4:1). He goes outside the city, makes himself a shelter and waits 'to see what would happen to the city' (4:5), apparently still hoping that God may see sense (!) and destroy these heathen enemies.

It is one thing to rebuke a fault; it is another to correct and set on the right track (see 2 Timothy 3:16). The negative attitudes have been dealt with, but the positive graces are not yet present. Jonah is still not in agreement with God. He does not see the Ninevites as the Lord sees them, or care for them as the Lord cares for them, and that is what the Lord wants from Jonah and from us. So God teaches him further lessons in order to bring Jonah into conformity to the heart and character of God — a remaking in the image of Christ.

The prophet, waiting to see what will happen, suffers discomfort from the heat of the sun, in spite of his shelter. So 'The Lord God provided a vine and made it grow up over Jonah to give shade for his head to ease his discomfort' (4:6). Then the Lord also provided a worm to chew the vine and so cause it to wither. After this the Lord yet again provided 'a scorching east wind', which combined with the blazing sun to make Jonah grow faint. Jonah was, inevitably, most upset. From this we learn two lessons with Jonah, first about himself and then about the Lord.

The vine and Jonah

We need not spend time discussing the exact nature of the plant — the vine or gourd — nor need we speculate about its amazing rate of growth. It is enough for our purposes to know that, as with the big fish, it was the Lord who provided it to further his own purposes. (Incidentally, we should note that not only the pleasant vine, but also the unpleasant worm and wind were 'provided' by the Lord in his sovereignty. We must beware of speaking of God's 'permission', as if he had no choice or merely fitted in with circumstances. In fact, he initiates the unpleasant action for his own good purposes.) Jonah initially suffers discomfort and then is delivered from his trouble by the Lord, only to be brought back into the first position by the death of the vine. The vine made Jonah 'very happy' (4:6), but the reversal of the situation made him want to die (4:8).

The parallel here is between Jonah and the Ninevites. Both were in need, although Jonah's situation was trivial by comparison with theirs. Nineveh was threatened with destruction; Jonah was merely suffering discomfort, but suffering nevertheless. Just as the Lord was gracious to Nineveh by forgiving the city in his grace, so he was gracious to Jonah in his need, even though he had not repented of his sin and resentment! Just as the Lord was patient with Nineveh, so he was patient with Jonah. Instead of punishing Jonah for his arrogant anger with God and his continuing hatred of the Ninevites in defiance of God, the Lord provided him with a shelter. Jonah, who has already experienced the grace of God in his deliverance from the sea through the fish, is shown once more that he, just as much as the Ninevites, deserves God's wrath, but has received only grace, mercy and forgiveness, symbolized by the vine. This makes him very happy; why then should he grudge the Ninevites their happiness? Are they not all in the same boat?

Then, if that is not enough, the Lord reverses the process. Having said, in effect, 'You enjoyed being sheltered from the sun and from my wrath; so do the Ninevites,' the Lord adds, 'How do you like it when I do to you what you wanted me to do to them, i.e. withdraw my forgiveness?' Jonah is given a taste of his own medicine and finds it very bitter indeed (4:8). He uses the same words as in verse 3: 'It would be better for me to die than to live.' First he was upset because they *were* spared; now he is upset because he is *not* spared. What a reversal! Surely now he can begin to see things from their point of view.

The basis for all this is startlingly simple. Both halves of his experience teach Jonah that he is a man just like the Ninevites. Part of a privileged race he may be; one of God's covenant people he is; a prophet of God he is called to be, but as a *man* he is no different from them. He, too, feels discomfort and pain; he, too, sins and needs grace; he, too, has feelings. The words in which Shakespeare's Shylock, the Jew, describes himself and his fellow-Jews express this fact from the opposite direction: 'Hath not a Jew eyes? Hath not a Jew hands, organs, dimensions, senses, affections, passions, fed with the same food, hurt with the same weapons, subject to the same diseases, healed by the same means, warmed and cooled by the same winter and summer, as a Christian is? If you prick us, do we not bleed? If you tickle us, do we not laugh? If you poison us, do we not die?' (*The Merchant of Venice,* Act 3, Scene 1). In Shakespeare's day it was the Jew who was regarded as being not really human — Antonio had called him 'dog'. In Jonah's day and later, it was the Jew who thought of the Gentile 'dog' like that. But both Jews and Gentiles are human beings, made in the image of God. Proverbs 17:5 puts this in its proper perspective: 'He who mocks the poor shows contempt for their Maker; whoever gloats over disaster will not go unpunished.'

During the great battle to end the slave trade, the potter Josiah Wedgwood designed a cameo showing a negro kneeling and pleading with the words: 'Am I not a man and a brother?' You do not have to be a brother in the deepest sense of being a child of God to be a brother-man. This would be the Ninevites' unspoken plea to Jonah through his experience with the vine: 'Learn how we feel; learn what it will mean for us to spend eternity in hell. Can you then refuse to feel compassion for us and leave us to our fate — a fate you would never be able to endure yourself?'

In just the same way, we, today, must realize that beneath all the differences of colour, culture and ability lurk human beings like ourselves. We must learn that opponents of God and enemies of ourselves though they may be, they are still people who can be hurt and suffer as we do. They may not see it that way themselves; they may despise us and our compassion, but the fact is that, however unpleasant and hateful others may be, they are human beings like us and our responsibility is to want for them what we want for ourselves. If you do not want to go to hell and suffer the eternal and excruciating torments of God's wrath, how can you wish it on anyone else? We condemn those who damn and curse others so idly and casually with their words; how then can we do the same, effectively, by our lack of compassion, lack of concern, lack of action? The next time you dismiss someone and think only of justice without mercy, put yourself in his shoes and say, 'He also is a man and a brother.'

The vine and the Lord

The next and final lesson follows in the last verses of the book, as the Lord draws attention to himself and his attitude to the city of Nineveh. Although Jonah has been rebuked for his callousness and been shown his oneness with the Ninevites, he could — and probably would — still bring his theological objection against the Lord. In the prophet's estimation, God ought to show his justice and vindicate the truth by punishing them; anything less is to deny hs own justice, as Jonah had feared all along. Now the Lord answers this too.

Jonah is angry about the vine which has given him shelter, not just because he has lost its help, but for its own sake. God has harmed this inoffensive and helpless plant and Jonah is angry with him, because he is 'concerned about' it. In verses 10-11 the Lord seizes upon this show of pity and concern, to make the point — *the* point of the book — about his own love, pity and concern for all men.

Jonah, the Lord points out, is concerned for the vine; he has an attachment to it, a Ninevite plant! This is a reflection of God's own attachment to men — all men, even Ninevite men. The character which Jonah describes so gloriously (4:2, borrowed from Exodus 34:6-7) is true of God's attitude to any and all men. His offers of mercy and forgiveness to all are utterly sincere.

This love is not the deepest kind of love — the electing love which God has set upon his chosen ones from eternity — but rather that mercy, love and compassion which God has for all his creatures. We can see the distinction in Ephesians 2:4-5: God is rich in mercy (absolutely), but 'his great love for us' is that specific love, which does more than offer mercy and express willingness to forgive — which actually redeems, calls effectively, rescues and saves. I make this distinction, not to limit or depreciate the love of which this book speaks, but simply to stress that while there is a greater love which only the elect know and experience, there is a genuine and wonderful love for all.

Some do not like to call this 'love' at all, reserving the word for God's love for his own people, and Jonah does not in fact use the word here. However, the rest of Scripture uses the word 'love' to express this 'common grace', this merciful attitude to unbelievers without distinction.

'The Lord is gracious and compassionate,
    slow to anger and rich in love.
The Lord is good to all;
    he has compassion on all he has made.
The Lord is righteous in all his ways
    and loving towards all he has made'

(Psalm 145:8-9,17).

This passage agrees with our Lord's own words in Matthew 5:43-48, that it is when we 'love' our enemies that we bear a childlike resemblance to our heavenly Father and behave after his pattern of doing good to both righteous and unrighteous. It is very sad that many feel they cannot preach and teach the sovereign electing and saving love of God without denying the reality of this general love. (It is also sad that even more cannot preach this general love without denying the sovereign, distinguishing love!)

This is probably the love spoken of in John 3:16 — a love which is for all without exception. It is possible to interpret that most famous of verses to mean that God loves the 'elect world' or to stress, with B. B. Warfield, that it is the sinfulness of man that is particularly in view in the term 'world' and so remove the issue of number. However, it is much simpler and, I believe, more consonant with the rest of Scripture, to take 'the world' here as meaning men without distinction and the love as that which provides a Saviour and sets him before all men, so that 'Whoever believes in him shall not perish but have eternal life.' Such a love, which is not the same as the eternal love which we can know is ours only after we have believed, is truly amazing. In this sense (but only in this sense) Christ became the Saviour of the world (John 4:42; 1 John 4:14) and the propitiation for the sins of the whole world (1 John 2:2). The sinner is to be told of a love of God for him, of a Saviour whom he can trust — a crucified Saviour — without bothering about the hidden intricacies of election and particular redemption. They are even more glorious in their place, but at this point the unbeliever and the Christian witness need to know about and base their actions upon the general love of God, which is the source of the offer of mercy in the name of God.

Put negatively, we must make sure that, like the Lord, we 'take no pleasure in the death of the wicked, but rather that they turn from their ways and live' (Ezekiel 33:11). On the contrary, we should rejoice with the angels in heaven — and surely with God himself is meant (Luke 15:10) — over one sinner who repents.

Why is this so? Why does God have this love and show this compassion to sinners? Why does he gladly spare those who repent? Verses 10-11 spell out the answer to this question, using a typical biblical 'how much more!' argument: 'If you, Jonah, have a concern for this plant, how much more ought I to have concern for the great city of Nineveh!'

The vine and Nineveh

The Lord's appeal to Jonah implies a series of contrasts. The first is this: *the vine is merely a plant; the Ninevites are men!* The vine is not even an animal (note the reference to cattle in verse 11). God cares, and we should care, for men simply as men, as people. What a devastating criticism of Jonah's attitude! He gets most upset about the vine, but would quite cheerfully consign the Ninevites to hell. This should come home to us. How many weep over the death or destruction of a favourite rose or a vandalized grape-vine, but are unmoved by considering the fate of men and women!

It has often been remarked that the British are a nation of animal-lovers and that the Royal Society for the Prevention of Cruelty to Animals is far better supported than the National Society for the Prevention of Cruelty to Children. This, in itself, is a national disgrace — to value animals above people, even at the earthly level, just as Jonah valued the vine above people. Further, we must consider how many Christians make great sacrifices for their pets and weep when they die, yet can see men and women slipping into hell with dry eyes!

On one occasion, driving over the moors to preach on, of all things, Jonah, I was saddened and quite upset by the sight of a dead lamb by the roadside. Certainly we should not be callous about the sufferings of animals, but I was convicted that I was far less troubled about the many unsaved sinners in the place to which I was going, than I was about that lamb. Jonah indeed! We must share God's tender compassion for men.

'Though he brings grief, he will show compassion,
    so great is his unfailing love.
For he does not willingly bring affliction
    or grief to the children of men'
(Lamentations 3:32-33).

Further, *the Ninevites had been created and nurtured by the Lord; Jonah had done nothing for the vine.* If, in spite of this, he cared for the vine, how much more would the Lord care for the people of Nineveh! God had made them, provided for them, nurtured and cherished them, but Jonah did not care.

We are reminded of God's rebuke to Baruch, Jeremiah's secretary: 'I will overthrow what I have built and uproot what I have planted, throughout the land. Should you then seek great things for yourself?' (Jeremiah 45:4-5). How can Baruch bother about himself and his prospects, when God's heart is breaking at having to punish his beloved ones? God's justice does compel him to punish, but he can only do it with a heavy heart. Yet Baruch's heart is light, as Jonah's would be and as ours too often is. The aborting of unborn babies in the womb distresses us terribly, I hope — the destruction, the horror, the waste of it all, after conception and growth and progress towards birth and a new person on earth. But the thought of men, with all God's care lavished on them over many years, going to destruction leaves us unmoved. Shame on us!

Again, *the vine was ephemeral; man is immortal.* 'It sprang up overnight and died overnight,' but the Ninevites, the Lord is implying, have 'a never-dying soul to save' (Charles Wesley). The idea of an immortal soul is not as popular with the theologians now as it once was, but whatever the technical arguments about the biblical terminology, the reality is clear. Man is made for eternity; he is destined for everlasting life or death, blessedness or torment. If Jonah is concerned over a temporary plant, how much more should he, and we, be concerned, as God is, for those who will exist for ever!

Christ reminded his disciples of their position in this respect: 'See how the lilies of the field grow. They do not labour or spin. Yet I tell you that not even Solomon in all his splendour was dressed like one of these. If that is how God clothes the grass of the field, which is here today and tomorrow is thrown into the fire, will he not much more clothe you, O you of little faith?' (Matthew 6:28-30). The same 'much more' should apply to our compassion for our fellow-men. If a wild horse were to trample down the flowers in our garden, we would be very upset, but the devil can 'steal and kill and destroy' and we do not care.

The Lord also points out that these people are unable to 'tell their right hand from their left'. This is often taken to apply to infants, but that would give an improbably high figure for the population of Nineveh. It is more likely to refer to them as *moral* infants, who could not distinguish properly between right and wrong. This is not to say, of course, that they had no moral sense or were morally not accountable; the guilt of the Ninevites was clearly established. Nevertheless, they were 'without law', without the benefit of that special revelation which Israel had received. They did not know much of the law of God, still less the gospel and, therefore, were to be pitied in their ignorance.

In the same way, Jesus, we are told, had compassion on the crowds, when he saw them 'harassed and helpless, like sheep without a shepherd' (Matthew 9:36), that is, without proper teachers to guide them. They were still guilty, but their condition under the false shepherding of the scribes and Pharisees aroused his pity. In the same way, we must have pity on those who have been brought up in 'heathen darkness', in our land as well as in lands far away. The vandals who disturb our rural or urban peace are not to be resented and rejected for their ignorant behaviour, but pitied for the lack of a Christian upbringing or even minimal religious instruction in school. Instead of despising those who have been led astray by false teachers, like the Jews of Christ's day, as 'this mob that knows nothing of the law' (John 7:49), we should be aware of their lack of privilege and opportunity compared with ourselves and pity them accordingly.

Add to all this the sheer numbers involved and the Lord's question, 'Should I not be concerned about that great city?' is truly unanswerable. Then it was 'more than a hundred and twenty thousand'; now it is the millions in our vast conurbations. It is often the crowds of people that arouse pity, as for our Lord on the occasion to which I have just referred.

Not only were the Ninevites men like Jonah himself, they were God's creatures made in his own image, made for eternity, made for communion with himself. As such they were beloved by God — the objects of his mercy and compassion and concern. So they must be objects of loving concern to Jonah; so their modern equivalents must be objects of loving concern to us. No matter what they are like — no matter how wicked, hateful, guilty, filthy, offensive or opposed — they are men, made by God, and we must have compassion on them. Far from delighting in their downfall, we must seek to win them for Christ and mourn deeply if they refuse God's overtures of peace.

Response

We are not told what Jonah's response was to the Lord's words. The impression is that he was left speechless. Perhaps he answered, in the words of Job on a similar occasion:

'I am unworthy — how can I reply to you?
    I put my hand over my mouth.
I spoke once, but I have no answer —
    twice, but I will say no more'

(Job 40:4-5).

As in some of Christ's parables, the story is left unfinished, waiting for the response of the hearers. Certainly here, the ball is left firmly in Jonah's court — our court. What will your response be?

We must all, I suspect, confess, if not to a total lack of

compassion, to selective compassion, as described in an earlier chapter. We sympathize with those whom we love or respect; we have pity on the weak and the struggling, the attractive and the decent, but those whom we count as enemies, natural or religious, those who have offended us or manifested open enmity against our Saviour, for these we have nothing but anger, a desire that they may get what they deserve. Far be it from us to offer them mercy, far be it from us to pray and long that these should escape the judgement of God.

If this is so, then the Lord must first deal with our simple rebellion against his revealed Word, for he has commanded us to show pity to all without exception. His chastisement may not be pleasant, but it is necessary and effective!

Next our pride must be removed, as he shows us once again that we too are saved only by grace, that we deserve mercy no more than these, who in many cases had far less opportunity and far fewer privileges than we did. If this is, indeed, the case, then we must remember once again, with Jonah, that salvation is from the Lord, and with Paul that 'At one time we too were foolish, disobedient, deceived and enslaved by all kinds of passions and pleasures. We lived in malice and envy, being hated and hating one another' (Titus 3:3). Who are we to look down on others and judge them unworthy of receiving eternal life?

Then we must begin to see them as real people like ourselves and understand their feelings, their needs and problems, their vulnerability and hopelessness. What we want for ourselves we must want for them also.

Finally, we must see them as God sees them and adopt his attitude too — one of love and mercy, of pity and compassion. We must have the mind of Christ, who was the friend of sinners and who died for those who opposed, persecuted and even killed him.

And then we must do something about it. Like Jonah, after the fish had vomited him up onto the dry land, we must take up once more our commission and go out to declare to the great city around us that they must repent and believe the gospel of God's grace, before it is too late.

III. Habakkuk and the holiness
of God

6.
Habakkuk's problem

Once again we have a prophet in difficulties. Once again we have to read the book as a whole before we get the answer properly; stopping part way can give us a distorted idea of the Word of God. In the case of Habakkuk both the prophet's understanding of his problem and the answer progress as we go through the book. Unlike Jonah, Habakkuk knows from the beginning that he has a problem and, also unlike Jonah, he immediately turns to God for the answer.

A two-fold problem

Habakkuk has a problem both with the situation in which he and Israel find themselves and also with the fact that God has not answered his prayer concerning this problem. Put in general terms, Habakkuk is troubled about the prosperity of the wicked. This is a common problem in the Old Testament, as it is also in Christian experience. The psalmist records:

> 'But as for me, my feet had almost slipped;
>   I had nearly lost my foothold.
> For I envied the arrogant
>   When I saw the prosperity of the wicked'

(Psalm 73:2-3).

Another Old Testament believer complains:

'You are always righteous, O Lord,
   when I bring a case before you.
Yet I would speak with you about your justice:
   Why does the way of the wicked prosper?
Why do all the faithless live at ease?'

                                      (Jeremiah 12:1-2).

Like them Habakkuk grieves over the state of Israel. The situation is within the nominal people of God. He cries out concerning 'violence' (1:2):

'Why do you make me look at injustice?
   Why do you tolerate wrong?
Destruction and violence are before me;
   there is strife and conflict abounds'

                                       (1:3).

Not only is there a failure of law and order, but the godly remnant is especially persecuted: 'The wicked hem in the righteous, so that justice is perverted' (1:4).

Thus the problem is not simply the age-old problem of evil in the world, but the state of the people of God — to us, the state of the church. In many ways Habakkuk's situation is our situation. It is true, not only in other lands, but in ours also, that the godly remnant is persecuted. This can show in two forms. In many lands, especially Communist or Muslim ones, the people of God are afflicted and tormented, both by injustice and by violence. However, the real issue in our society is where the godly within the nominal church are subject to trials from the official church. The evangelical minority is criticized and often placed at a disadvantage. We are despised, denied privileges and often made to feel that we are not really part of the church at all.

Behind this lies the deeper trouble that grieves the prophet so much. Why is it that the people of God are in this state? Why is it, we may say in our day, that the church is so ungodly, that the gospel is not believed or preached in most places of worship? Why is it that God allows his name to be dragged in the mud and his truth to be despised? Why is it that the power of the Spirit is lacking and revival tarries? Why is it that, while we do our best and try our hardest, relatively little is achieved? And so the complaint could go on. The only parts of the evangelical church that seem to prosper at all are those that deny the historic truths and pander to the ways of the world and the spirit of the age.

All this is not just an intellectual problem for Habakkuk or for us. It has driven him to earnest prayer, but he has received no answer:

> 'How long, O Lord, must I call for help,
>   but you do not listen?
> Or cry out to you, "Violence!"
>   but you do not save?'
>
> (1:2).

Like the psalmist he has prayed: 'It is time for you to act, O Lord, your law is being broken' (Psalm 119:126). And like him he could no doubt say, 'Streams of tears flow from my eyes, for your law is not obeyed' (Psalm 119:136).

So today, in spite of the accusations of some and the apathy of many, it is a fact that many are troubled by the state of affairs. There are many who hold to the doctrines of grace, who believe in the power of God to save and to transform the church and who have prayed and do pray earnestly for the Lord to act. We see the situation worsening in our land; we see the church losing numbers and power and the evangelical church becoming more and more taken up with trivialities and pleasure. We see evangelism turned into pop concerts and rock entertainment, and we sorrow and plead. But all the time the situation appears to get worse. What should we do?

A first response

The one thing Habakkuk does not do is give up praying or give up hoping. It is because he still trusts God that he takes his problem to God; it is because he trusts that his question is not simply 'Why?' but 'How long?' The issue is not whether or if God will work, but when. Again the psalms show the same attitude: 'How long will the enemy mock you, O God? Will the foe revile your name for ever?' (Psalm 74:10). 'How long, O Lord? Will you be angry for ever? How long will your jealousy burn like fire?' (Psalm 79:5).

It would seem that our Lord had this kind of situation in mind in that perplexing parable found in Luke 18:1-8, the so-called parable of the importunate widow and the unjust judge. The theme is not just prayer, but the prayer of those who are afflicted by those in power and authority. It is 'justice' for which the widow pleads, for vindication from her adversary. The Lord's assurance in verse 8 that God will see that his chosen ones get justice, 'and quickly', is followed by a question: 'However, when the Son of Man comes, will he find faith on the earth?' This has raised many problems over the years, but for our purposes the point is surely this: that it is not God's willingness to hear and answer that is in question, but our faithfulness and perseverance in prayer.

So, like Habakkuk, we must have both this holy impatience and persevering faithfulness. The first stage of this is that we shall take our problem to the Lord, for he does answer. The answer we need is not a fresh revelation, but an understanding of what he said to his prophet so long ago. However, we shall not gain this understanding unless our approach shares the prophet's realization of the situation, his grief over it and his deep concern that something should be done. As with Jonah, we are not concerned with mere answers to questions; we are in the business of changing the situation.

7.
God at work

Sometimes we talk of 'an amazing providence' — a striking intervention in our lives by God himself. It is to such an intervention that the Lord directs the prophet's attention in verse 5 of the first chapter:

> 'Look at the nations and watch —
>   and be utterly amazed.
> For I am going to do something in your days
>   that you would not believe,
> even if you were told.'

This is God's first answer to Habakkuk's problem and, although there is much more to follow, the basic solution to his perplexity in the face of the prosperity of the wicked is found here: an understanding of, and faith in, the providence of God.

The specific event to which the Lord refers is an invasion by the Babylonian army, but as we apply this to ourselves we must see this in the setting of the whole of God's providence. Remember that in the book of Jonah God 'provided' not only the big fish to rescue that prophet and the vine to give him shelter, but also the wind that scorched him and the worm that destroyed the vine. God 'works out *everything* in conformity with the purpose of his will' (Ephesians 1:11). So, if we want to lay a proper foundation for dealing with this particular problem of the apparent triumph of evil and the low state of the people of God, we must come to an understanding of the ways of God, so far as they are revealed to us.

God does work in the world

Verse 5 teaches us to look behind the appearances, whether of our own lives, or of international affairs as in this passage, to see the hand of God. Everything is under his control; life is not just a matter of cause and effect. Although, of course, we can trace the human origins of many things that happen, we have to accept that God brings everything to pass.

On the one hand we must reject deism, that philosophy/theology of the eighteenth century which shut God out from the world he had created, by seeing him just as a creator who set things in motion and then withdrew into masterly inactivity. As Jesus himself said, in John 5:17, 'My Father is always at his work to this very day.'

On the other hand, we must dismiss the idea, so current in evangelical circles, which conceives of the so-called 'god of the gaps'. This is not confined to ideas about creation, where God is allowed a small and ever-decreasing amount of space for activity where natural causes seem to fail; it also includes those who limit God's activity to the marvellous and miraculous. Let us be quite clear. God is in control of everything; his sustaining power underwrites everything. Without him nothing would exist or function at all.

This means that even where men think they are in control, God in fact brings about his will and purpose. Thus, in verse 11, the Lord refers to the way the Babylonians attribute their success to their own military power — 'Whose own strength is their god' — but it is all his doing. See also Proverbs 16:1,9:

> 'To man belong the plans of the heart,
>   but from the Lord comes the reply of the tongue...
> In his heart a man plans his course,
>   but the Lord determines his steps.'

This truth is vital for our peace of heart and mind in times of perplexity, and for our hope in times of trouble. No matter what man decides, no matter what circumstances seem to dictate, no matter what our weakness may seem to render inevitable, nothing can happen to us apart from God's providence and that, we know, is always for our good. When we quote Romans 8:28 about 'all things' working together for our good, we must have no exceptions whatsoever. This is also the foundation for our prayers. We are praying to the one who actually works in the world. We do not believe in the power of prayer itself; we believe in the sovereign providence of the one to whom we pray.

Incidentally, it is vital that we include in this sovereignty all matters to do with salvation. There are many who willingly talk of God being 'still on the throne', about all things working together for good, but who then exclude salvation from God's domain. Here alone, it is said, God has left his throne. Here man reigns supreme; his free will *finally* decides whether he is saved or not. God can only stand by and wait. How God can ordain and order everything else in eternity, while he has to wait for man to decide on his response to the gospel is beyond me. The only way to honour and trust God's sovereign power and care is to exclude absolutely nothing from it. God's providence is the outworking of his predestination in every sphere, including eternal life.

God works in an amazing way

For much of the time God works in what we may call an ordinary way, a regular way — so regular that men can talk of 'the laws of nature'. If this were not so we would be in a very difficult position. Not only could we have no weather forecasts, but we would be unable to act with any confidence in the ordinary matters of life. However, sometimes, and especially in connection with the welfare of his own people, God works in a very surprising manner. Often this has been a matter of miracles; more often it is what we may call special providences — events which are surprising in some ways, but which do not represent an extraordinary use of God's power.

Here he says that he is going to work in a way which is not merely surprising, which could never have been forecast, but which is frankly inconceivable! Israel, God's chosen people, is to be punished (see 1:12). Here, then, the amazement is because they are ignorant of God's ways, for he had in fact made it perfectly clear that if Israel sinned she would be chastised. Psalm 89:30-37 draws attention to the 'fine print' of the covenant made with David, that if his descendants departed from God's ways, they would be dealt with severely. This should not have been surprising, but it was.

However, on other occasions, God's ways take us by surprise

simply because of our ordinary human ignorance. We must not make God in our own image, as does one theologian, who ought to have known better, when he wrote recently, 'God maintains control over what happens, not through the unfolding of a predetermined plan, but by waiting and watching for things to happen, by extemporizing in a series of makeshift and emergency provisions.' On the contrary, that is how man tries to keep control, but fails.

That is why God so often takes us by surprise. We do not know what he knows; we have no idea what God's plans and purposes are, unless he, on rare occasions, reveals them; we are ignorant of his aims and so the outcome often amazes us. Frequently, our surprise comes because we either do not know or do not remember the power of our God. We do well to notice the description of God in Ephesians 3:20 as the one 'who is able to do immeasurably more than all we ask or imagine, according to his power that is at work in us'. The suddenness of revivals in the past has often led the saints to speak of God's works in terms of Isaiah 66:8:

'Who has ever heard of such a thing?
    Who has ever seen such things?
Can a country be born in a day
    or a nation be brought forth in a moment?'

It is this confidence in the surprising work of the God of the impossible that we need in circumstances like Habakkuk's.

God works through rulers

It is not just ordinary individuals through whom God works. This passage is full of references to the Babylonian nation and to their and others' rulers (1:10). 2 Chronicles 36:17-22 directs us to God's sovereignty over sovereigns! God, we read, 'brought up against them the king of the Babylonians... God handed all of them over to Nebuchadnezzar,' and then later, 'In order to fulfil the word of the Lord spoken by Jeremiah, the Lord moved the heart of Cyrus king of Persia to make a proclamation throughout his realm and to put it into writing' for their return from exile. Truly, 'The king's heart is in the hand of the Lord; he directs it like a watercourse wherever he pleases' (Proverbs 21:1).

What greater encouragement could have been given to Habakkuk, if he had eyes to see it in the midst of the invasion? The same God, who brought down the Babylonians on them in judgement, was also able to take them away again. History is full of illustrations of this principle. Spurgeon tells of a Dutchman called Oncken who braved the wrath of the local mayor, who had threatened him with death, asserting that unless God permitted, he could do nothing at all to him. The same King Henry VIII of England who persecuted William Tyndale for translating the Scriptures into English was brought to authorize the publication of that very Bible with the memorable words, 'Let it go forth.'

We have no need to fear the powerful and influential. In fact, the New Testament commands us to pray for them in order that God's people may live in peace and holiness (1 Timothy 2:1-2). Whatever the situation, whatever the persecution and opposition of rulers, our God is able to change it. He who brought it can take it away again. In every case our comfort and hope depend on believing and knowing that God is in control even of rulers and even of those opposed to him.

God works even through the wicked

The description of the Babylonian army given in verses 6-11 is frank and terrifying; the Lord stresses their ruthlessness, fierceness and cruelty:

'Their horses are swifter than leopards,
    fiercer than wolves at dusk.
Their cavalry gallops headlong;
    their horsemen come from afar.
They fly like a vulture swooping to devour;
    they all come bent on violence'

(1:8).

Can such warriors be the instruments of God? How can we reconcile this with God's purity and justice? The answer to that comes later, but for now we must simply consider the fact.

According to Proverbs 16:4, 'The Lord works out everything for his own ends — even the wicked for a day of disaster.'

Isaiah puts it slightly differently:

'I form the light and create darkness,
    I bring prosperity and create disaster;
I, the Lord, do all these things'

(Isaiah 45:7).

A failure to accept this ruins all comfort and destroys hope. We must believe that even the wicked are under God's control, or there is no assurance that he will ever be victorious. Perhaps, we would say, the devil might win in the end; perhaps evil might go on prospering and wicked men go on being violent. Even Satan is subject to this. Even he is used to further God's holy purposes. In the words of the Puritan William Gurnall, 'God puts his eggs under the devil for him to hatch!'

We have to go further than saying that God permits evil and wickedness. There is a difficulty here, since we cannot, and must not, say that God is responsible for sin, but we have to go further than mere permission, as if God were forced to allow wrong, or merely bringing good out of evil, as if God were making the best of a bad job. God exercises his sovereignty in such a way that man's responsibility is not removed and God's character is not sullied. These Babylonians whom God is 'raising up' (1:5) are described in verse 11 as 'guilty men'. Each has his own responsibility; God is sovereign, but man bears the sin.

The difference is in the intention. Joseph's brothers sold him into slavery sinfully, but it was all in God's hands and in God's plan. Joseph is not afraid to say in Egypt, 'God sent me ahead of you to preserve for you a remnant on earth and to save your lives by a great deliverance. So then, it was not you who sent me here, but God' (Genesis 45:7-8). 'You intended to harm me, but God intended it for good,' he adds in chapter 50:20. If any doubts remain, then the cross should end all dispute. Judas bore the responsibility even though the crucifixion had been prophesied and was thus part of God's eternal plan: 'The Son of Man will go just as it is written about him. But woe to that man who betrays the Son of Man! It would be better for him if he had not been born' (Matthew 26:24).

This assertion in verse 5 of God's impending sovereign action was clearly aimed at the rest of the nation: 'you' is plural. Acts 13:40-41 applies this to 'scoffers', who would appear, in Habakkuk, to be those who did not care about the situation. They are the sinners who are basically responsible for the judgement that is coming upon the nation. If they do not repent then they will suffer in that judgement. So the warning comes for us. Are we ready to acknowledge our sin, our responsibility for the present poor situation, or are we just ready to complain?

Chiefly, however, we must apply this to Habakkuk. The Lord's first response to his questioning is to assure him that, despite all appearances to the contrary, he, the Lord God Almighty, has everything in hand. Even though the first result of Habakkuk's prayer will be, apparently, to make matters worse, he must trust God, who works in the world to fulfil his own purposes.

8.
Habakkuk's God

Sometimes people refuse medical treatment because it seems to them, often with some justification, that the cure is worse than the disease. They would rather go on with their illness than submit to the somewhat drastic measures prescribed for their relief. They are not willing to trade the possible alleviation of their disease for certain loss of hair and other traumatic side-effects. This could well have been Habakkuk's reaction to God's answer to his prayer.

Verse 2 records his plea for God to help, but the situation, in fact, is made worse. He asks God to save them from the violence that surrounds them, but the Lord's reply is to send more and greater violence in the shape of the Babylonian invader. Such a terrible onslaught and destruction is foretold that he must have wondered whether the nation could survive. Were God's people doomed? Was there no hope? Well might he have used the words of the prophet, 'How can Jacob survive? He is so small' (Amos 7:2).

We, too, have to wonder whether the church can survive. The devastation seems no less, even though we may remember that it is God's judgement upon sin. We are in the middle of it and we wonder how much longer we can survive if God continues to chastise the nation and the nominal church — and us with them. We have no exemption from the afflictions that are coming on our nation, our civilization and culture. If AIDS, or more precisely, the immoral and reprobate way of life that has hastened and spread this plague, is the judgement of God, as Romans 1 makes clear, we in the church are not immune from the effects.

Habakkuk, however, knows the answer to this difficulty. True, he will only come up against another problem, from verse 13 onward, but thus far, at any rate, he knows what he has to say and do.

We must remember God

'O Lord, are you not from everlasting?' is not a doubting question, but a confident assertion in the form of a question. It is an appeal: 'You are from everlasting, aren't you? And, therefore, certain things are true for us.' He knows his God and knows to turn to him, no matter what the trouble may be. That means knowing the character and being of God, knowing his promises and purposes in so far as he has revealed them. A failure to remember who and what God is lies at the root, not only of much faulty action, but even much faulty prayer. Theology matters — applied theology, that is — and especially in the strict sense of teaching about God himself.

We can take an example from the collects of the Church of England Prayer Book. We may not like the set forms, but Cranmer's theology of prayer, as revealed in these forms, is worth noting. Most of these collects begin with a description of God himself, in terms clearly related to the request that is to be made. Thus, one of the best known and loved of these prayers begins by reminding us that God has 'caused all holy Scripture to be written for our learning' and then asks, appropriately, that he will 'grant that we may in such wise hear them, read, mark, learn and inwardly digest them that by patience and comfort of thy holy Word, we may embrace and ever hold fast the blessed hope of everlasting life, which thou hast given us in our Saviour Jesus Christ'.

So Habakkuk piles up names and titles of God to remind himself of the Lord's attributes and attitudes, which are so relevant to his case. First, he declares God's majesty, glory and power: he is 'from everlasting', unlike both men who oppose him (1:11) and idols, who support the enemies and to whom his own people might be tempted to appeal. He is the 'Lord', the self-existent and unchanging one, who revealed himself to Moses at the burning bush as the Sovereign One, able to redeem and deliver his people. He is the 'Holy One', not just in terms of sinless purity, but in terms of Isaiah's vision in chapter 6 of one 'seated on a throne, high and exalted, and the train of his robe filled the temple', above whom the seraphs were 'calling to one another, "Holy, holy, holy is the Lord Almighty; the whole earth is full of his glory."' How often we evacuate these terms of their glorious meaning and then wonder why we have no faith to pray or to persevere!

Then the prophet calls to mind God's covenant faithfulness, first by the use of that word which is vital in any context, 'my'. He is *'my* God'. The very term 'Lord', also, is so often used with the implication of the covenant of grace behind it. This is the God of his people Israel and of individual Israelites — and our God also. This is the God of the promises, the one who is committed to them and to us. In some ways even more startling is the expression *'my* Holy One'. No one is surprised if you refer to 'my dog', but how startled they would be if you mentioned 'my mammoth'! There is something of the same shock involved in saying, 'my Holy One'. How can he speak of a God of such majesty and awe-inspiring holiness as 'my'? He is not, of course, speaking in any possessive way, as if God were instantly available for his use, 'on tap' as it were. Nevertheless, he is speaking of one whose holiness is exercised on behalf of his servants and whose majesty confounds all their foes.

He also refers to the Lord as the 'Rock', one who is sure and reliable in every stormy situation, one who is sure in his ways and certain in his defence of his people. Toplady's familiar 'Rock of Ages' is the God of Isaiah 26:4: 'Trust in the Lord for ever, for the Lord, the Lord, is the Rock eternal.' In gospel terms, we may add,

On Christ, the solid Rock, I stand,
All other ground is sinking sand.

and may rest secure on the knowledge that

We have an anchor that keeps the soul
Steadfast and sure while the billows roll,
Fastened to the Rock that cannot move,
Grounded firm and deep on the Saviour's love.

Once we have remembered our God, then we can and must draw the proper deductions from his being and character. This Habakkuk is not slow to do, for it is from this that he gains all his assurance in the face of impending disaster.

We can and must trust God

In the midst, therefore, of all the distress, both present and future, Habakkuk is confident in the Lord. God is still the same, still able and willing to help, so he commits his cause to him. He does not run away in rebellion; he does not retreat into his shell in sullenness; he does not lose hope. Instead of turning away, he appeals to the everlasting God, his God, and so has peace. The problem has not gone away, but at least he has reminded himself that God is in control and that he is his God, with the best interests of Habakkuk and the rest of the people at heart. So, he can come to the confident conclusion: 'We will not die.'

He knew that God would not allow his people to be wiped out. The words of Jeremiah 30:11 are clear:

> '"I am with you and will save you,"
>   declares the Lord.
> "Though I completely destroy all the nations
>   among which I scatter you,
> I will not completely destroy you."'

In Malachi 3:6 this certainty is grounded on the unchanging character and purposes of God: 'I the Lord do not change. So you, O descendants of Jacob, are not destroyed.' God's purposes of good for his people — and we should add, his purposes of grace for his elect — demand that the nation survives. The onslaught of the Chaldeans is part of the age-long struggle between the seed of the woman and the seed of the serpent, which is to come to a head in the battle between the incarnate Christ and Satan, and which the seed of the woman is destined to win. Therefore, it is not possible that the covenant people should be wiped out; it is not feasible that God's promise of a Saviour should be rendered impossible and ineffective.

No matter how far the Lord permits and ordains the attacks of the enemy to succeed, his purpose will never be thwarted. Habakkuk need not, and does not, fear the outcome, however traumatic the immediate future may be. There will always be a faithful remnant, however small. The conclusion of Isaiah chapter 6, which is so often ignored, confirms this. Isaiah, who willingly accepts the commission of God to preach his Word, is then told that it is a message of judgement and defeat. However, he is assured that 'As the terebinth and oak leave stumps when they are cut down, so the holy seed will be the stump in the land.' We, today, have no cause for despair, even though at times the remnant seems desperately small. God's final purposes depend for their fulfilment on the continued existence of the people of God. As long as we maintain a faith like Habakkuk's in the everlasting grace and power of our Rock, we need not be afraid.

The prophet can, however, go even further and comes to his confident and quite amazing conclusion: 'O Lord, you have appointed them to execute judgement; O Rock, you have ordained them to punish' (1:12). At first sight this seems like a contradictory confession of despair, but it is not. Jeremiah 30:11 is again of help and gives us the clue: 'I will discipline you but only with justice; I will not let you go entirely unpunished.'

There is no room for complacency, no justification for ignoring the sin of the people, but nevertheless the punishment is not that of final rejection, but of fatherly correction and chastisement; it is discipline. Habakkuk, at this stage, has no idea of what the Lord is actually doing, but he is clear that all is in his hands, that he knows what he is doing and where he is going, and therefore the prophet can be quietly confident.

The essential thing for the remnant is to be 'exercised' by their condition. We must not despair and give up the struggle, but nor must we sit back in over-confident ease. The Lord is disciplining us and we must take it to heart. For the nominal church and the unbelieving churchgoer, the present troubles may be final rejection. For those who love the Lord and his Word it is a time for reflection and repentance. Can we say that we are free from sin? Do we believe that it is only the hypocrites with whom God is displeased? Dare we acquit ourselves of all responsibility for the state of the church?

It may be that we have not given up belief in the doctrines of the faith; we have not relaxed our moral standards. But where is the zeal and compassion we ought to have? Are we truly and earnestly prayerful? Is our godliness anything like that of our forefathers? The mark of the remnant is that the punishment and discipline which God brings upon his church bears fruit. 'No discipline seems pleasant at the time, but painful. Later on, however, it produces a harvest of righteousness and peace for those who have been trained by it'(Hebrews 12:11).

The Lord will not destroy his people, whom he has chosen and called. He is going to fulfil his purposes and this purifying and training is to equip us for the day of his power. We must understand where God is going, even though we cannot know the details. We are to repent, to learn, to obey and work. We must be laying foundations for the future, so that the work, when it comes, will not be superficial and feeble and ephemeral. If we trust God, our God, in all that he is doing now, then we shall be prepared for what he will do in the future. This much, at least, Habakkuk knew: God had only purposes of good for his people, and for his prophet among them. So he would trust, even where he did not understand.

There is, today, no room for despair. Despair enervates; it removes all incentive to work, all stimulus to prayer. What we need is not a foolish optimism that thinks that all will be well, just because we are hoping for the best, but a certain trust in the gracious character and purposes of our God. This being so, we shall do what we can now and prepare for a brighter future — 'as bright as the promises of God'.

9.
The problem of evil

The prophet started with the problem of God's apparent inactivity and unconcern in the face of rampant evil. To this the Lord gave his answer, in verses 5-11, with the prophecy of the Chaldean invasion to chastise the sinful nation. This raised another issue — that of the danger to God's people in this invasion, but to this Habakkuk himself provided the answer. He knew his God and his promises, and, therefore, knew that the nation would not and could not die, that the Lord was chastising and disciplining his own people for their good and for the ultimate securing of his plans.

However, this only raised a third problem for the much-tried prophet. (Incidentally, is it not true that the only Christians who do not have problems are those who refuse to think honestly about life?) How do you reconcile such evil with the God of the Bible or, as it is often put, with a God of love? Many today raise this issue immediately when confronted with the gospel message. They point to war and suffering, to grief and famine, and contend that it is impossible to reconcile all this with any idea of a God of love. Either he can do nothing about it, and so is not really God at all, or he chooses not to, and is not the kind of God they want. What do we say?

In one sense this is a digression from our main theme, but it comes up inevitably as Habakkuk works things out before God. Too often, Christians have no proper answer to the whole issue that Habakkuk faces, because they cannot accept this element in the picture. In any case it is such a common difficulty, sometimes assumed by unbelievers as a defence, but often real, that we shall do well to follow Habakkuk as he probes the issue.

Verse 13 states the problem in its starkest form:

'Your eyes are too pure to look on evil;
     you cannot tolerate wrong.
Why then do you tolerate the treacherous?
     Why are you silent while the wicked
swallow up those more righteous than themselves?'

If God is so pure, as he surely is, how can he allow the Babylonians
to do their worst? How can he actually use them as his instruments
of justice and discipline? Man cannot touch pitch and not be defiled;
is God exempt from this contamination?

Habakkuk is not alone in asking this question in the Scriptures.
Asaph too, in Psalm 73:2-3, had to face up to this. Indeed, he almost
lost his faith over it, as he records:

'But as for me, my feet had almost slipped;
     I had nearly lost my foothold.
For I envied the arrogant
     when I saw the prosperity of the wicked.'

How should we respond? How did Asaph and Habakkuk? How easy
it is to weaken and give way to the opposition by denying the facts
— by lowering our idea of God and his ways! This is not the way,
as Habakkuk demonstrates in the following verses, before going on
to a more positive stance.

We must not deny the suffering

We are not engaging in a philosophical discussion of the origin and
nature of evil or even of sin. We are facing the issue of personal
suffering, the sort of thing that Christians and non-Christians have
to face in their own lives as well as in the experience of others. This
is the sort of situation that pastors have to deal with week after week.
The world is full of wickedness and suffering. Habakkuk is quite
clear that the Babylonians are 'wicked' (1:13,15), that the nations
are suffering like fish caught 'without mercy' (1:17). He makes no
attempt to avoid the issue; indeed, it is real for him personally, not
just for a possible objector.

The last thing we must do is to minimize the suffering in order to 'let God off the hook'. It is easy, in our attempt to justify God, in our legitimate concern for his reputation, to become harsh and callous, to be unfeeling in the face of extreme misery. We can be guilty of a lack of compassion, indeed of apparent cruelty, which hardly commends the gospel we are seeking to advance.

Job's friends did this, when, in order to defend the justice of God, they invented sins for Job and his sons (Job 8:4; 22:5). They did not actually deny or minimize his sufferings, but the effect was the same; they had no sympathy with him and it showed. It may be quite true that the worst aspects of famine in India could be alleviated if the cow were not regarded as sacred because of false religion and if it could be killed and eaten, instead of taking up much of the food that is available. It may well be true that the effects of famine in some countries could be relieved, but for the sin of man in civil war. But we must not spend so much energy on denouncing man's inhumanity to man, in order to excuse God, that we have no time or emotional resources to do something at least to help the sufferers. It may be their own fault; it may not. We are to represent a gracious and compassionate God and do what we can to lighten the sufferings, no matter what has caused them.

One of the great merits of the Scriptures is that they constantly face the facts, instead of looking the other way, like so many of us do. The wicked often do prosper. They do end their days in peace, and their children inherit their ill-gotten gains. Honesty is not always, from a human perspective, the best policy. Accept this, with all its perplexity and, although you may not understand the plight of the sufferer, you can at least actively sympathize with it and try to help.

We must not deny the sovereignty of God

This is a frequent error, especially among Christians who are themselves deeply compassionate or over-anxious to remove a stumbling-block from the path of a potential convert. We can sympathize with both categories, but this is not the right way to solve the problem. As I have already mentioned, it may be true that much of the trouble can be traced to man's sin and inhumanity, but not all. There is also the malign influence of Satan to be taken into account. However, when all is said and done, there remains a large amount of suffering, such as the effects of storms, earthquakes and disease, that cannot be blamed on man. Still further, we find that the Bible quite clearly lays everything that happens, whether good or evil, including the first category, ultimately at God's door.

Habakkuk, in this passage, while speaking of the depredations of the Babylonians, for which he holds them responsible as 'wicked' men, says to the Lord, '*You* have made men like fish in the sea' (1:14). In verses 5 and 6, the Lord himself says, 'I am going to do ... I am raising up'. Man's sin and Satan's enmity are part of the answer and it is right to point this out on occasion. Finally, however, the buck stops, not on the president's desk, but at the throne of Almighty God. Contemplating the ruins of God's own city, Jerusalem, and the terrible sufferings of princes, 'hung up by their hands', and compassionate women, who 'have cooked their own children', the author of Lamentations can still say,

> 'Who can speak and have it happen
>   if the Lord has not decreed it?
> Is it not from the mouth of the Most High
>   that both calamities and good things come?'
>
> (Lamentations 3:37-38).

The fact is that, although denying God's absolute sovereignty seems a good way out, it really destroys hope. If God is in no way responsible, then he cannot do anything to help either. If this tragedy has happened in spite of him, then it is out of his control and we are left without comfort or encouragement. A young couple were, understandably, devastated by a second tragedy in their family. The mother was angry and tended to blame God, but in spite of this, constantly looked to God for help. The husband did not 'see what God has to do with it ... It's just one of those things.' He did not blame God, but he left himself without help and hope in his situation. There is a way to answer the complaint, as Habakkuk ultimately shows, but if you shut God out, this answer is not available and you are left on your own. Habakkuk did not fall into this trap. Because of this, at a later stage, he finds hope.

We must not deny the justice of God

It seems that to deny that God is just is the only option that the prophet has left. The suffering is real; God is the Lord indeed. So, if he is involved with all this injustice and cruelty, it must cast the gravest doubts on his integrity and fairness and purity. There would be no problem if the Lord were merely like the gods of the heathen: vicious, arbitrary and cruel, sporting with mankind as mere play-things of their whims.

That, however, is a conclusion Habakkuk cannot accept. His God, as he says in verse 13, has 'eyes ... too pure to look on evil'. That is not open to question. The problem is to reconcile the character of God with the facts. It is only when you try to believe in the God of the Bible that there is any problem! Jeremiah found himself in the same predicament. In chapter 12:1, he complains,

'You are always righteous, O Lord,
   when I bring a case before you.
Yet I would speak with you about your justice:
   Why does the way of the wicked prosper?
Why do all the faithless live at ease?'

Those who deny the sovereignty or justice of God have no difficulty. God is simply wrong or helpless. Habakkuk and Jeremiah are not at liberty to come to either of these conclusions, and nor are we. Asaph, in Psalm 73:13, is perplexed similarly and almost says, 'Surely in vain I have kept my heart pure; in vain I have washed my hands in innocence,' but he does not. He will not 'betray this generation of your children'; he will not speak like an unbeliever. Sadly, too many Christians today do just that. They deny God's lordship or his justice in practice by their complaints, if not in theory. All the biblical authors with problems at this point refuse to take the easy step of denying that God is just. Abraham speaks for the rest in Genesis 18:25: 'Will not the Judge of all the earth do right?' The question answers itself. If God is not a just judge he is not really God at all.

The contemporary form of this complaint is more often put in terms of God's love, but it amounts to the same thing. God should not be doing or allowing what he is! Therefore, we will not believe on him or we will not serve him. (Rarely do men see the contradictory nature of their complaints. They reject God's existence because of the cruelty and suffering they see in the world; but if God does not exist he is not responsible for it, so it is no ground for rejecting his being!)

If we do reject these ways out of the difficulty, what do we say? How do we quieten our hearts? How does Habakkuk answer his own dilemma?

We must trust God

The prophet turns to God with his problem. How foolish to keep on turning it over in his feeble mind when he can seek the face of the Lord and look for his answer! So he does just that. In verse 1 of chapter 2, Habakkuk declares his intention to 'stand at [his] watch'. He will wait in humble submission for God to answer. 'I will look to see what he will say to me.' Here is the proper humility before God which we find at the end of the book and the trial of Job. God manifests himself in his glory and power, and Job, in effect, says, 'Who am I to question God? What am I to object to God's ways?' Habakkuk does ask the question, but it is in submission, not anger, with a readiness to hear, not to protest.

There are the beginnings of an answer here. Later verses explain more as the prophet listens, but the first thing to do is to quieten your spirit before God. 'He is right. I can trust him. I will stop complaining; I will cease worrying. I will simply wait for God. In his own good time he will make all clear, or it may be I shall never understand. So be it. I will still trust God and give up my resentment and the pride that fosters it.'

Habakkuk also recognizes that God has not finished yet. He believes, not only in the sovereign power of God, which can do something, and in the justice of God, in spite of appearances. He also believes that God has not finished his purposes. There must be an answer, even if he cannot fathom it. Perhaps the answer lies in future action. So in verse 17 he uses the crucial words, 'keep on', just as the psalmists ask, 'How long?' 'Is he to keep on emptying his net, destroying nations without mercy?' Indeed, later verses do tell him that God's judgement awaits the wicked in God's time. Jeremiah, again, has the key:

'The fierce anger of the Lord will not turn back
   until he fully accomplishes
the purposes of his heart.
   In days to come
you will understand this'

(Jeremiah 30:24).

But for the moment Habakkuk has to be content with waiting submissively.

The words of Psalm 131 are appropriate here:

'My heart is not proud, O Lord,
   my eyes are not haughty;
I do not concern myself with great matters
   or things too wonderful for me.
But I have stilled and quieted my soul;
   like a weaned child with its mother,
like a weaned child is my soul within me.
   O Israel, put your hope in the Lord
both now and for evermore.'

Pending a final, or further answer, we can say with the psalmist,

'My flesh and my heart may fail,
   but God is the strength of my heart
   and my portion for ever.
Those who are far from you will perish;
   you destroy all who are unfaithful to you.
But as for me, it is is good to be near God.
   I have made the Sovereign Lord my refuge;
   I will tell of all your deeds'

(Psalm 73:26-28).

Should we then expect direct answers from God in our troubles? Will God speak directly to us so that we can say, 'God has told me what to do'? No. We must remember that Habakkuk was a prophet. His experience, like Hosea's, was not just for him, but for others. Thus we must note that he is looking, not just to see what the Lord will say to him, but also to see 'what answer I am to give to this complaint'. This refers to his prophetic office. He must give an answer to those who question him. He must pass on God's message to those who complain. We are not in his position, but in theirs — dependent on the Word of God, as given, in part, through him.

1 Corinthians 10:11 tells us that these things were written for our instruction and warning. Indeed, 'It was revealed to them [the prophets] that they were not serving themselves but you, when they spoke' (1 Peter 1:12). Instead of looking for new revelations and fresh answers to our problems in our times of trouble, we should look more closely at what God has already said, the answers he has

already given. In this case, we must take to heart what the prophet was taught, and in the first place that means being quiet before God and waiting for him to show us his will through his Word, rather than demanding that he do what we want.

One last comment has to be made at this point to those who are still impatient for God to end the suffering and stop the troubles. One element in God's delay, in his apparent toleration of evil and wickedness, is his infinite grace and mercy and longsuffering. He is giving them time to repent. The message of Jonah must be incorporated into Habakkuk. If God's judgement were to be poured out on all those who at present deserve it, who would stand? How many of those who complain against the injustice and lovelessness of God would regret their haste, when his wrath came upon all sinners, not just the cruel and arrogant, but also the decent but ungodly!

10.
Waiting in faith

The Lord is answering Habakkuk in stages — dealing with the prophet himself, as much as with the problem. As we consider the revelation of chapter 2:2-4, we are reminded that there is a vast gulf between the theoretical problem of suffering and the practical issue of *my* sufferings. In our last chapter we were thinking about the former; now Habakkuk is instructed about the response he and his fellow-believers ought to make in their own situation.

The temptation is to give up and give in. Job's wife urged him to do this: 'Are you still holding on to your integrity? Curse God and die!' (Job 2:9). Even the psalmist reached this point in his trial:

'Surely in vain I have kept my heart pure;
   in vain have I washed my hands in innocence.
All day long I have been plagued;
   I have been punished every morning.
If I had said, "I will speak thus,"
   I would have betrayed your children'
(Psalm 73:13-15).

But he did not. He drew back from the brink. Habakkuk, too, must beware of this, so the Lord, before coming to the next stage of the answer to the problem itself, instructs the prophet and the rest of the righteous how they must react in the present situation.

This is a vital lesson for us all to learn. We must realize that the Lord frequently has to deal with us spiritually, as he did with Jonah, before we are able to accept his instruction about individual problems. The answers that he gives are intelligible and acceptable only to those who have been chastened and refined by the Spirit's dealings with their souls. We must learn, in cases like this, to make haste slowly. The method is all-important. As we follow the Scriptures we are often told to slow down — to take a long, hard look at ourselves — and then, in due course, God will make things clear.

> God is his own interpreter
> And he will make it plain
>
> (William Cowper).

Sometimes, of course — and this is true in this particular case of the problem of evil and suffering — there is no final intellectual and theological answer accessible to our weak and sin-affected understandings. In such cases it is even more important to hear what the Lord is saying to us and about us, rather than demanding answers to our problems. The Lord has, in fact, much more to say about Habakkuk's problem, but we must take note first of what he is saying to us personally.

'The righteous,' the prophet is told, 'will live by his faith' (2:4). In the New Testament these words are quite correctly applied to justifying faith (Romans 1:17; Galatians 3:11), but also to persevering faith (Hebrews 10:37-39). There is, of course, no contradiction. The two 'kinds' of faith are continuous. Faith is a trust in, and a commitment to, God and his Word in every form and at every point. The righteous is justified by the same faith that continues and keeps him faithful to his God and thus righteous in practice. This is one of the clues to the doctrine of final perseverance: all who are truly justified will persevere, since the same faith that received justification will also hold on to the Lord in persevering obedience. Here, it is the latter application of faith that concerns us. It is seen in all three verses and Habakkuk's instructions are equally relevant to us as we face trials and sufferings.

We must treat God's Word seriously

Faith in God includes faith in his Word — in this case, the revelation given to Habakkuk. This revelation is to be written down and made plain, partly because it is not just for him alone, as we saw in connection with verse 1. The reading and running of verse 2 have caused some perplexity. Keble's hymn version, 'There is a book, who runs may read,' is not very helpful! The true idea seems to be that the message must be written down plainly, not so that someone running by is able to read it, but so that one, who is to read it aloud, may run with it and read it to the righteous. In other words, it is vital that God's people in times of trouble should have the Word of God. It is urgent; the herald must 'run', not saunter.

This is their life-blood in their distress. This was true for the psalmist: 'If your law had not been my delight, I would have perished in my affliction' (Psalm 119:92). It has equally been true for all the persecuted in every age, including our own. Christians imprisoned for their faith have longed for the Bible that has been taken from them; they have searched their memories for every verse which will feed their souls and comfort them in their trial. It is for this reason that such efforts have been made to get the Scriptures into lands where the saints are persecuted. Their need is not just theoretical teaching; it is strength and enabling in deep trouble.

How vital it is that we should learn this lesson! It is no good having an answer for those who argue about the problem of suffering, if, in our own time of difficulty, we do not know where to turn. If you would have faith in God, turn to his Word. Listen to the herald, as he reads out God's message: 'The righteous will live by his faith.' This is the way for those who would continue to be righteous in the midst of the storm.

We must wait for its fulfilment with patience

One of our chief troubles is self-inflicted. We cannot or will not wait patiently. We demand an immediate answer; we want the fulfilment of God's Word instantly, on a par with our desire for instant coffee! Usually, however, God's people have to wait for the realization of their hopes and expectations. Whether it is Abraham waiting for a son, the Jews looking for their Messiah or Christians longing for the coming of the Lord, patience is required. So, Habakkuk is warned that the fulfilment of the revelation he is to receive has to await the 'appointed time', that it may linger.

This is hard to accept. It is all right in theory; it is simple to see it in the Bible or to tell others, but a different kettle of fish when it is the end of *our* suffering that is postponed, the termination of *our* trial that is delayed. Nevertheless, patient we must be. This is where faith comes in. The prophet is given guarantees that the fulfilment will happen, even though not immediately, but even without knowing just what this means, he has to trust God. He must remind himself, as Billy Bray would have said, that 'Father knows best'. He must be prepared to wait in the confidence that if he had his way it would not work out right, that if he allowed his impatience to control him it would spoil what God had prepared for him. God's wisdom is true; our wisdom is derivative at best and unwisdom at worst. Later on Habakkuk will receive instructions as to how he should spend his time while he waits. For the moment it is sufficient that he is told that God's will is that he does so, no matter how hard it is — no matter how bitter the experience, how painful the trial.

There must be no panic, no despair. Abraham, when he agreed to Sarah's suggestion that he lie with Hagar, was really yielding to panic. 'Time is getting on. I am getting older. If nothing happens soon, it will be too late.' So he left the path of faith for the time being and went along the way of the flesh. Others do not panic; they simply despair; they give up walking in the way that God has set before them.

Both these tendencies are evident today. It may be the Christian who yields to the temptation to blame God for the continued suffering of himself or a loved one, or the minister who undergoes a crisis of confidence in the tried and trusted, biblical ways of evangelism and church-building, and goes in for gimmicks and carnal efforts to succeed at any price. Patience implies the awareness that in the end the promise will be kept, deliverance will come — an awareness which keeps us on the right path of faith. And this awareness the prophet is given.

We must trust the promises of the Word

As I have stated already, the prophet is assured that the fulfilment is certain, that though it delays, it 'will not prove false', 'it will certainly come and not delay'. Instead of thinking merely of what we desire, we must learn to see it as God's purpose. We must realize that the word 'end' implies a planned goal, not just a finish. God is working out his purpose; he is doing something definite and we shall not be let down if we trust him. The fulfilment may 'delay' from our standpoint, but it will never be 'late' — the better translation — according to God's timetable.

Patience does not mean mere resignation. The waiting is not to be in inaction and silence. We must go on praying in faith while we wait, just like Elijah, who had been promised rain, but went on praying until the cloud actually appeared. The strength to do this comes from faith. 'Live' does not just mean go on existing; it is an active word, a positive word. Just as in Romans 1:17 it implies the gift of eternal life and in Hebrews 10:38 means to be 'saved' (see verse 39), so here it promises life and blessing. Not only will Habakkuk be spared the judgement that will fall upon the wicked; the fulfilment will be worth waiting for. It will come as the gift of life out of death, blessing after suffering, vindication after mockery and scorn. At present it is hard, if not impossible, to see this, but then it will become very clear.

Psalm 73 puts this beautifully. After the doubts and near despair expressed earlier in the psalm, Asaph declares,

'I was senseless and ignorant;
    I was a brute beast before you.
Yet I am always with you;
    you hold me by my right hand.
You guide me with your counsel,
    and afterwards you will take me into glory.
Whom have I in heaven but you?
    And earth has nothing I desire besides you.
My flesh and my heart fail,
    but God is the strength of my heart
and my portion for ever'

(Psalm 73:22-26).

On either side of the promise about the righteous in Habakkuk 2:4, we read about the wicked, who is 'puffed up', whose 'desires are not upright', and this leads into the assurance that he and those like him will be judged (2:5-20). Habakkuk, by contrast, will enter into the large and abundant blessing that God has prepared for him — by faith. So the warning is given: do not envy the wicked and, above all, do not join them. The temptation is always there. David makes this quite clear:

'Do not fret because of evil men
   or be envious of those who do wrong;
for like the grass they will soon wither
   like green plants they will soon die away'

(Psalm 37:1-2).

No matter how perplexed you may be by the present victories of the wicked, no matter how painful may be your experience of the triumph of evil men in your personal life, in your local church or in the wider condition of Christ's people, do not despair, do not give up, but trust God. He has said that his purposes of good will mature and his promises will be kept. His revelation will come to pass in due season. Your task is to wait in faith. And to do this you need to take his Word seriously and believe his promises. We need more than a philosophical answer to the problem of evil. We need a faith that will keep us walking in righteousness and unto life.

11.
The final answer

In the course of our consideration of Habakkuk's questioning we have digressed slightly into the area of the problem of evil in general. As we come to God's final response we must return to the narrower issue of the condition of the people of God. Habakkuk's particular concern was the apparent triumph of God's enemies over his own people — for us, the failure of today's church, which should trouble us just as much. So far God has explained to the prophet that he is using the Babylonians to discipline his own people. Habakkuk is assured that God is still the everlasting Rock of Israel and therefore they will not die. Now, having made the point forcefully that the righteous must persevere in faith if they would live in the fullest sense of that word, the Lord comes to the climax of his dealings with the prophet.

The Babylonian enemy will be judged and destroyed

Chapter 2, from verse 4 onwards, gives a detailed description of God's coming judgement on the Babylonian king, who is the epitome of the unrighteous one mentioned in verse 4. The five woes are a taunt of ridicule and scorn from the peoples that he had previously taken captive (2:5). This is simply a way, not of warning the Babylonians — who would not hear this message — but of encouraging the righteous in their life of faith. Those who have been plundered by the Babylonian king will plunder him in turn (2:6-8); those who have been ruined will cry out for judgement, which will come (2:9-11); all his labour to establish his city will be to no purpose for,

> 'Has not the Lord Almighty determined
>   that the people's labour is only fuel for the fire,
> that nations exhaust themselves for nothing?
>
>   (2:13).

What an encouragement this is for us who feel ourselves to be so small and weak against the powerful enemies of the truth, against the forces of the world, with all their resources of money, influence, control of the media, etc! Though for a time they may prosper and the church will be subject, as it is at present, the time will arrive when all this will come to nothing. In God's time, according to his determination, the powers of the world will fall and even be taunted by those who were held in slavery. All their efforts to abolish and eliminate the church of God will be seen to be fruitless. As so often in the past, the church will still be found alive when tyrants and ideologies have passed away.

The tiny, infant church in Madagascar suffered twenty-five years of brutal persecution by Queen Ranavalona from 1835 to 1861. Missionaries were banished and the few young Christians seemed doomed to extinction. However, when the queen died, the church emerged from the furnace larger and stronger than before. Much more recently, while Communist dictatorships have been falling all around the world, the church that they tried to destroy is still in existence and, again, even stronger than before.

We must take heart from this to go on in faithfulness and righteousness. There is too much pessimism and even despair in the Christian church today, even among evangelicals. We must have confidence that the devil's subtle weapons of heresy and worldliness can no more defeat God's church than his cruder tool of persecution. Truly, the 'nations exhaust themselves for nothing' (2:13) against the church that Christ is building, whatever the appearances may be today.

However, the message is not merely a negative one; it is not just a declaration that the enemy's purpose will be frustrated. There is also here a positive declaration in verse 14 and on this we must spend some time.

God's glorious purpose will be fulfilled

The Babylonian king's purpose will get nowhere in the end. His schemes will all fail, but God's eternal purpose is sure. The promise of verse 14, 'For the earth will be filled with the knowledge of the glory of the Lord, as the waters cover the sea,' is so all-embracing that we must look to the eternal kingdom for its complete fulfilment. That, however, does not prohibit us from using it to encourage hope in the present. Clearly this prophecy was intended to raise the hopes and hearts of Habakkuk and the other righteous ones. The defeat of Babylon is seen as the necessary first step in the complete and glorious victory of the people of God, the universal spread of the knowledge of the Lord. This saw its great step forward in the coming of Christ and the establishing of the New Covenant. The calling of the Gentiles through the ministry of the believing remnant of the Jews is included in this vision. How could this be if the nation were to be destroyed in Habakkuk's day?

Virtually the same prophecy completes Isaiah's vision of the coming up of 'a shoot ... from the stump of Jesse' (Isaiah 11:1,10), the birth of the great Son of David, the incarnation of the Son of God. The assurance of these prophecies is that the very character of God's kingdom is one of growth and spread, of an extension to the ends of the earth. The words of the Lord's Prayer, 'Your kingdom come', unite with the Great Commission to 'go and make disciples of all nations' (Matthew 28:19), to encourage us to believe that God is going to bless our labours and not allow us to be wiped out.

Just how much will be seen before the Second Coming is no clearer than just how much will be true at any one time, but the intention of these words in Habakkuk is to lift the spirits and encourage the persevering witness of the faithful. We should take them in the same way. As we look at the present situation, we should gaze beyond it to the fulfilment of God's purpose. Notice the 'for' in verse 14. That is the guarantee of the defeat of the enemies God's people actually faced. If these enemies were to be victorious then God's plan could not come to fruition. Therefore, they cannot be victorious; it is impossible. The same is true today. If our enemies can finally destroy the church, if they can really triumph, then God's purpose is forfeit. That is unthinkable. Such is not, and cannot be, the case.

God's judgement is sure

As the first three woes declared the inevitable failure of the
Babylonian plan, so the last two set out God's certain judgement
upon them. This again is a guarantee that they cannot finally destroy
Israel. The fourth woe, verses 15-17, makes clear that when the
persecutor has finished his unintended work of disciplining and
refining the people of God, it will then be his turn to suffer
judgement. He has caused Israel to drink from the cup of God's
wrath, but now it is his turn: 'The cup from the Lord's right hand is
coming round to you, and disgrace will cover your glory' (2:16).

The fifth woe (2:18-19) shows why this must be. It is because
they trust in idols, in 'an image that teaches lies', instead of the living
God.

> 'Woe to him who says to to wood, "Come to life!"
>   Or to lifeless stone, "Wake up!"
> Can it give guidance?
>   It is covered with gold and silver,
> there is no breath in it.'

One is reminded of the scathing words of Psalm 115:3-8:

> 'Our God is in heaven,
>   he does whatever pleases him.
> But their idols are silver and gold,
>   made by the hands of men.
> They have mouths, but cannot speak,
>   eyes, but they cannot see.
> they have ears, but cannot hear,
>   noses, but they cannot smell;
> they have hands, but cannot feel,
>   feet, but they cannot walk;
> nor can they utter a sound with their throats.
>   Those who make them will be like them,
> and so will all who trust in them.'

By contrast God's judgement is certain and final, because he is
the true God. The final verse of chapter 2 calls all men — both
Habakkuk and Babylonians, both enemies and servants — to

worship the Lord: 'But the Lord is in his holy temple; let all the earth
be silent before him.'

As in Psalm 46:10, 'Be still, and know that I am God,' the main
call is to the rebel to submit in silence, but God's people, too, must
observe this. There are to be no ungodly questionings and complaints. In the end Habakkuk must put his hand to his mouth and be
silent like Job:

> 'I am unworthy — how can I reply to you?
>   I put my hand over my mouth.
> I spoke once, but I have no answer —
>   twice, but I will say no more'
>
> (Job 40:4-5).

The temple referred to here is clearly the heavenly one, as in
Jonah 2:7, the eternal dwelling-place of the great God of all the
earth, where he has his throne. There he reigns and from there he
issues his judgements. Here we face God, the sovereign Lord:
sovereign to ordain, sovereign to command and sovereign to judge.
Our contemporaries do not, on the whole, worship gods of silver and
gold, but there are many — even professing believers — whose God
is not sovereign like this. He has to bow to man's free will; he has
to permit evil that he cannot control; he waits for men to let him help
them. Such lack of belief in a real God is a recipe for doubts and
problems, a certain way of producing debates and arguments with
the Lord and complaints about his dealings with us — all far
removed from verse 20 and all leading to despair and hopelessness
in our difficult situation.

In the end this vision of God in his glory upon the throne is the
answer to all the problems. He it is who rules, not evil kings, so do
not fear. He uses nations to discipline his erring people, but is not
dependent on them and will judge them in their turn, so do not
despair. He has the right to do as he wills, so do not rebel or
complain. Resist every temptation to murmur or complain, to
question or doubt. He will work out his glorious purpose, no matter
what men may do, so have faith. He demands your obedience and
service, so go on in righteousness.

Habakkuk's problems of mind and heart are dealt with, but there
is more to come. There is a positive answer to be heard.

12.
Prayer for revival

The temptation is to stop at the end of chapter 2. The Lord has answered the prophet's questions and objections. He has dealt with the intellectual and theological aspects of the issue — the prosperity of evil men — and even confronted Habakkuk with his lack of faith. What else is needed? What more can be required?

That is mere intellectualism — a failure to apply the truth practically. What is needed is for something to be done about the present situation. This remains unchanged. The diagnosis is clear, the disease has been given a name, its origin is clear and the blame rightly apportioned, but evil is still triumphant, the enemy is still in control and threatening to wipe out the people of God completely. What should the prophet do? He cannot just sit and wait; he cannot just let the situation go on, but what is there that he can do, for his best efforts are of no avail against such a powerful enemy?

The same question faces us today. We may realize that evil is victorious because of the sins of our fathers and of ourselves. We may be quite clear that God is not at fault and is in no way to be criticized; his sovereign power is undiminished, his love for his own undimmed, his hands are clean, his judgement of the wicked certain. But we still have empty churches and an unbelieving public outside; we still have heresies abounding and superficiality everywhere. God is still not glorified in the earth and our hearts are breaking because of this, or should be. What shall we do? Just wait? Or give up?

Habakkuk's answer is a prayer, to which God responds with a vision of encouragement, all enshrined in a psalm — a psalm which, according to verse 19, is intended for all to share in. The prayer and the encouragement are for us all.

A prayer to be copied

Habakkuk's prayer is brief and to the point:

> 'Lord, I have heard of your fame;
>   I stand in awe of your deeds, O Lord.
> Renew them in our day,
>   in our time make them known
>   in wrath remember mercy'

(3:2).

Simply to pray for renewal (3:2) in our day is to ask for trouble! But merely to pray for God to revive his work can be equally unwise. Without explanation these words are liable to be misunderstood and only unprofitable confusion will result. Debate over the subject of revival and renewal cannot be settled by the word itself, for it is simply a form of the verb 'to live'. It may mean, here, to make alive, to keep alive or to bring to life, i.e. create.

What does the context have to say? The work for which Habakkuk pleads is clearly one of mercy (3:2), so the renewal or revival for which he pleads is that of God's saving work among his people, which will result in God's fame being known more and more. The deeds of which he stands in awe are God's great deliverances of his people, not just the prophesied work of judgement on the Babylonians, but all the blessings of God's presence and power. The vision which follows refers back to the great redemption at the exodus, which confirms this.

If we bear this in mind, we shall not interpret revival, in a biblical sense, as being a mere evangelistic effort, as some do. We are not called to 'hold a revival', using a special 'revival pack' of decision cards etc., as advertised in the religious press. Nor can the idea be limited to a mere accession of new converts. In some cases this may be all that is required; the church is orthodox and earnest, but unsuccessful. Then the Lord provides his Spirit's power in convicting and saving sinners. Such events in the history of the church have been called revivals (sometimes local revivals), but surely much more is meant here.

The people of God are in a dreadful state — truly one of spiritual death (1:2-4), apart from the minute remnant of Habakkuk and the other 'righteous'. There has been sin; God is angry with his people and is chastising them. What is needed is a great work of transform-ation, life from the dead, indeed. The nature of a revival depends on the depth and character of the death that exists beforehand. Usually it is inadequate merely to pray for power, for conversions, however much we long for these. Much more is necessary before the church arrives at that point. Sadly this is not often recognized.

From this perspective, such events as the exodus; the return from exile (the giving of life to the valley of dry bones, Ezekiel 37); the outpouring of the Spirit at Pentecost, which transformed the people of God from a dead Pharisaic nation, with only a tiny remnant of believers, into the powerful church of Christ spreading the gospel to the whole world; the great work of the Reformation which changed the medieval, Roman church into the living Protestant and Reformed church; the Evangelical Awakening of the eighteenth century, which, before it saved many souls, changed the face of the church from within — all these were revivals.

And what we need today is not just power for our evangelism to be successful, but a far-reaching and thoroughgoing transformation of the whole church. For such a work of God Habakkuk was praying and for such a work of God we should be praying today. The nation was in a state of death; so is the church today. The nation was hopeless and helpless; so is the church today, in spite of superficial signs of activity, which some mistake for life.

What is needed is a return to biblical doctrine, a regaining of biblical priorities in faith, holiness and evangelism, a reformation of church practice, and then, in God's mercy, we may see a powerful spreading of the gospel which will transform society itself and lead to an even greater extension of God's kingdom across the world.

In fact, although the overall situation remains desperate and the outlook bleak humanly speaking, as superficiality seems to increase — and God's people are glad to have it so — there is also a recovery in progress in certain circles. The core remnant is being strength-ened, however slowly and gradually. There are some who have returned to the faith of their fathers and the practices of the great people of God, at least in some measure, and it does no honour to God and gives no help to the earnest believer to ignore or deny it.

It may well be that, although the storm is still raging and gaining most of the attention, the tide has changed and almost imperceptibly is coming in. God has, perhaps, begun to reverse the trend and change the situation. Let this be an encouragement to more fervent prayer.

Prayer for revival now

Habakkuk asks God to do this reviving work 'in our day', 'in the midst of the years' (AV). God can do this, however unlikely it may seem to us. It is possible for God, not only to begin a work in secret at any time, but even overnight to transform the whole state of affairs. In Isaiah 66:8 the Lord asserts his ability to do remarkable things:

> 'Who has ever heard of such a thing?
>   Who has ever seen such things?
> Can a country be born in a day
>   or a nation be brought forth in a moment?
> Yet no sooner is Zion in labour
>   than she gives birth to her children.'

We may apply to this difficult task what the Lord says in Isaiah 49:6:

> 'It is too small a thing for you to be my servant
>   to restore the tribes of Jacob
>   and bring back those of Israel I have kept.
> I will also make you a light for the Gentiles,
>   that you may bring my salvation to the ends of the earth.'

Indeed, if the Lord could do this amazing thing of bringing the Babylonians on them in judgement, why should he not be able to do a good thing in the same way?

> 'Look, at the nations and watch —
>   and be utterly amazed.
> For I am going to do something *in your days*
>   that you would not believe
>   even if you were told'
>
> (Habakkuk 1:5).

Those of us who have recently witnessed the amazing political upheaval in Eastern Europe — a reversal that no one could or did foretell — should not doubt God's power to do a similar but greater work in the spiritual realm, to overturn the kingdom of Satan in our land and 'in our day'. Preachers have often been mocked for their repeated use of the phrase, 'in this our day and generation'. But that is precisely what Habakkuk asked for and what we must look for.

Ask for mercy

In all this Habakkuk does not forget that it was the sin of the people that brought about this terrible situation — both the death of the nation and the consequent judgement upon them through the Babylonians. So it is for 'mercy' that he pleads. He acknowledges God's wrath; he does not deny their sin, but asks that God will nevertheless be merciful. The Old Testament is full of this principle. The Lord promised the people, through Isaiah:

'For a brief moment I abandoned you,
　　but with deep compassion I will bring you back.
In a surge of anger
　　I hid my face from you for a moment,
but with everlasting kindness
　　I will have compassion on you,
　　says the Lord your Redeemer'

(Isaiah 54:7-8).

The book of Judges shows a repeated cycle of blessing — sin — chastisement — repentance — deliverance. Daniel, in chapter 9, confesses the sins of the people, the sins of the fathers and his own sins, as he pleads for God to show mercy for his own sake.

This is a difficult lesson for us to learn. We have no right to be revived; we have no claim upon God's power and might. All the promises have been forfeited, if he should desire to be strict. It is not enough to plead with God for revival. No amount of all-night prayer meetings will be of any avail unless God is willing to listen, willing to be merciful and to forgive our sins. Listen to the author of Lamentations: 'Even when I call out or cry for help, he shuts out my prayer' (Lamentations 3:8). Later in the chapter he says,

'You have covered yourself with anger and pursued us;
　　you have slain without pity.
You have covered yourself with a cloud
　　so that no prayer can get through'

(vv. 43-44).

How can we expect God to come to us, to come down like fire from heaven, when we refuse to admit our fault, when we take pride in false teachings and ungodly practices, and flatter ourselves that really we are doing quite well? 'In wrath remember mercy' must be our cry. And the plea for mercy must be accompanied by genuine repentance — a change of mind and heart that leads to a change of practice.

God gives a vision to encourage us

The subject of the vision in verses 3-15 is God himself. The pictorial language of verse 3, 'God came from Teman, the holy one from Mount Paran,' recalls Deuteronomy 33:2:

'The Lord came from Sinai
  and dawned over them from Seir;
  he shone forth from Mount Paran.'

This refers to the exodus, when the Lord 'came' (acted) to defeat his enemies and deliver his people. Other verses, such as verse 11, call to mind the days of Joshua, when God caused the sun and moon to stand still in response to the prayer of a man.

Like the psalmist, Habakkuk is made to think of how God has worked in the past, as an encouragement for the present:

'I will remember the deeds of the Lord;
  yes, I will remember your miracles of long ago.
I will meditate on all your works
  and consider all your mighty deeds.
Your ways, O God, are holy.
  What god is so great as our God?
You are the God who performs miracles;
  you display your power among the peoples.
With your mighty arm you redeemed your people,
  the descendants of Jacob and Joseph'

(Psalm 77:11-15).

The relevance to the present day — for both Habakkuk and ourselves — is seen most clearly in the words of verse 6:

> 'The ancient mountains crumbled
> and the age-old hills collapsed.
> His ways are eternal.'

This God still comes to deliver as he did in the past; his ways are eternal. So, like the psalmist, we should learn and meditate about the past: the Old Testament, the New Testament and the history of the church. This will stir us to long for 'the years of the right hand of the Most High' (Psalm 77:10) and to pray for their return, believing that God can and does work in this way still.

Habakkuk's vision not only assures him of God's character as a delivering and eternal God; it adds the reminder that God comes and delivers in fulfilment of his covenant and his promises. Why does he do these great things? (3:8). It is not because he is angry with the rivers or the streams, but because of his covenant: 'You came out to deliver your people, to save your anointed one' (3:13). The 'us' of verse 14 is Habakkuk's assurance that he and the godly remnant are God's own people and that therefore he will rescue them.

So we must pray with confidence. Our God is still that eternal God who revealed himself to Habakkuk. He is the same God who rescued Israel from Egypt and delivered Joshua from the Amorites and whose covenant is everlasting. Still he comes in glory and splendour to rescue his anointed, Christ, and his people. Though we may ask only for mercy, we may do so in certainty that God is merciful to his people in spite of their deserts, and that he acts as their Deliverer in every age.

If we understand the present in terms of the problem of evil and suffering, if we have hope for the end in terms of the promise of the universal kingdom of God, then we must pray earnestly for the immediate future in terms of God's commitment to his covenant people. Do not complain, do not despair, but also do not resign yourself to a life of failure and misery. Pray Habakkuk's prayer with Habakkuk's faith on the basis of Habakkuk's vision of the living and eternal and faithful God of the covenant. Surely the Lord will hear such prayer.

13.
Meanwhile...

Habakkuk has one remaining problem: what should he actually do in the situation? The issues of justice, deliverance, faith and prayer have been settled, but how should he behave while the evil times persist and prevail? In verses 16-19 of chapter 3, he contemplates the continuing and worsening state of affairs. True, God is going to do something about the sin of Israel, by bringing the discipline and chastisement of the Babylonians on them, but as the army approaches it seems that the cure is worse than the disease. Although he anticipates 'the day of calamity' which will 'come on the nation invading us', before that happens there will be days of terrible distress for the land.

Invading armies, then as now, wreaked havoc wherever they went. The land would be laid waste, the flocks and herds killed, the crops in the field and in the vineyards destroyed. Verse 16 tells us of Habakkuk's reaction to what the Lord has revealed of the immediate future. He is no stoic, unmoved by the thought of suffering and distress:

'I heard and my heart pounded,
   my lips quivered at the sound;
decay crept into my bones,
   and my legs trembled.'

Then come the wonderful words of faith: 'Yet I...' In spite of all that is coming and in spite of his fear, he will not crumble; he will not collapse. He will persevere. By the grace of God, as he looks at the situation with honesty — as he refuses to hide his head in the sand — he insists that he will survive.

To us also this is a vital question. In the words of Francis Schaeffer's book, *How then should we live?* It is essential that we do not misjudge our God; it is essential that we look to the future for his deliverance and pray for revival. But what about now? What about tomorrow, when the pressures of life come upon us with renewed strength? What about next Sunday, when we feel more keenly than ever the spiritual devastation around us and the helplessness of the church? Can we, in spite of everything, still say, 'Yet I...'?

Some survive by refusing to consider the facts. 'Things are not so bad,' they say. They rely upon triumphalist reports of evangelistic missions that are always a huge success, of missionary work that never knows a reverse, of churches that never see defeat or division, and go on being cheerful simply by ignoring reality. This was not Habakkuk's way. He faced the facts of an impending invasion and could still say that he would not give in or despair.

It is not merely that he has prayed, not just that he has faith for the future. Here are the fruits of faith in the present, while he waits for God to remove this threat and thus renew his work in the midst of the years. Similarly, we must not merely pray for revival and ignore our present duty. So let us ask, 'What is it that the prophet was able to do because of his faith and confidence in a sovereign God?'

He had peace in the midst of distress

This, of course, can apply to our personal and family life, as well as to the life of the church, with which we have been chiefly concerned. The source and the expression of this peace are just the same. Because of our faith we can afford to 'wait patiently' or 'quietly'. We can have peace about the most desperate situation and wait without panic or complaint. We can apply the words of Philippians 4:6-7 to the church's hour of need, just as we would to our own hour of grief or perplexity. We 'present [our] requests to God', in this case that he will revive and renew his work, that he will keep us safe and help us, and then we can have that 'peace of God which transcends all understanding'. True, this is the outworking of our belief in God's sovereignty, care and ability to fulfil his glorious purpose. Nevertheless peace does not automatically come to those who know these things. This is, by definition, a peace that is not natural, but the special gift of God according to his promise and we should trust him to give it to us.

Nor is this an excuse for sitting back and doing nothing. Rather it is the basis for action. Only when we are at peace within can we go on with the battle without. It is not for nothing that Paul tells the Christian soldier to have his feet shod 'with the readiness', or preparedness, 'that comes from the gospel of peace' (Ephesians 6:15). The man who is overwhelmed with sorrow and worry because of the troubles of the day and the hopelessness of the cause will be of little use in the day of battle. Therefore let us consciously and deliberately seek this peace, so that we may wait for God in humble quietness, ready for obedient action as he directs.

Habakkuk also had joy in the midst of tribulations

To have peace is good, but it may be merely negative. According to Nehemiah's words to the Israelites who had returned from exile to embattled Jerusalem, 'The joy of the Lord is your strength.' Habakkuk declares that he will rejoice and tells us why in verses 17-18:

> 'Though the fig-tree does not bud
>   and there are no grapes on the vines,
> though the olive crop fails
>   and the fields produce no food,
> though there are no sheep in the pen
>   and no cattle in the stalls,
> yet I will rejoice in the Lord,
>   I will be joyful in God my Saviour.'

Once again he says, 'Yet I...' This is joy in spite of the situation.

All the usual means of joy dry up — food and clothing for Habakkuk, for us sound preaching, good fellowship, large congregations, the encouragements of conversions and the spread of the gospel. Nevertheless he will rejoice and so must we. This can be, not because we keep a stiff upper lip or pretend that these things do not matter. It can only, finally, be because we do not *depend* on these things for our joy.

In ordinary circumstances we gain joy from them. We are not

supposed to despise God's blessings, the normal sources of human or spiritual joy. But when these wells dry up we must still be able to rejoice, for we have a source that can never dry up, a well that never runs dry, a never-failing spring which flows whatever happens — our unbreakable relationship with God. Paul tells his readers to 'Rejoice in the Lord *always*' (Philippians 4:4), and that is what Habakkuk says he will do.

No matter what else may be true or what else may happen, the Lord — note the covenant name of the unchangeable, self-existent God — will still be his God. Nothing can alter this and that is the greatest possible source of joy.

> Though vine nor fig-tree neither
> Their wonted fruit should bear,
> Though all the field should wither,
> Nor flocks nor herds be there,
> Yet God the same abiding,
> His praise shall tune my voice;
> For while in Him confiding,
> I cannot but rejoice

(William Cowper).

Further, God is his Saviour; nothing can alter that either. Even though the heavens fall, God's people are still chosen, justified, reconciled, children of God and co-heirs with Christ, destined for eternal life. Temporal sources of joy can disappear for a time or even permanently, but the eternal ones nothing can touch, never mind destroy. So let us rejoice in this, or better in him, without ceasing.

Practically this means that instead of panicking, instead of rushing around like distraught chickens, instead of resorting to unscriptural gimmicks to try — vainly — to ward off the attacks of the devil or remove the chastisement of our God, we should seek his face in communion and love. More and more we should learn what it means to be the covenant people of the living God, what it means to have God as our Saviour. Meditation and communion with the Lord are not a form of escapism, a diversion from the serious business of the church, but the source of joy which is our strength in the day of battle. If we have this joy and look forward to that final salvation with certainty, we shall not easily give up the fight or despair even in the darkest days. Learn to rejoice in God, when the outward forms are gone and the usual means of grace are denied or deficient, and you will stand firm as Habakkuk did. This leads inevitably and finally to Habakkuk's last assertion.

He would receive strength in the midst of enemies

God gives strength to fight. Habakkuk is not simply to wait quietly in peace and joy. He is not just to pray that God will renew his work. When the enemy draws near he is to fight! The sequence is understanding — faith — peace — joy — strength for the battle.

> 'The Sovereign Lord is my strength;
>   he makes my feet like the feet of a deer,
>   he enables me to go on the heights'
>
> (3:19).

Psalm 18 is a psalm of battle as David takes confidence in the Lord who is his rock, his fortress and deliverer. Verses 32-35 help us to understand the meaning of Habakkuk's assertion.

> 'It is God who arms me with strength
>   and makes my way perfect.
> He makes my feet like the feet of a deer;
>   he enables me to stand on the heights.
> He trains my hands for battle,
>   my arms can bend a bow of bronze.
> You give me your shield of victory,
>   and your right hand sustains me;
>   you stoop down to make me great.'

Whatever the nature of the battle that he must fight — physical or mental or spiritual — Habakkuk is assured that he will be surefooted and swift in battle like a deer. He will take possession of the commanding heights of the country. Present-day Israel refuses to give up the Golan Heights because they command the dangerous border country. So Habakkuk relies on God's enabling for the battle ahead, confident of all the strength he needs to fight for the Lord.

When we see the devastation of Christ's church in our day, when we see the evidence of God's chastisement in the victories of modernism and every other kind of 'ism', we should not just sit down and cry. Nor should we only pray for revival, vital though that is. We must fight in God's strength against heresy and ungodliness — in ourselves as well as in others. We must fight positively in seeking holiness and reformation in the church, and especially in proclaiming the gospel of God's saving grace with all our might. God, who gives us peace and joy, will also give us strength for the fight and the ability to keep our feet and control the commanding heights, if we go forward with a faith like Habakkuk's.

The psalm and the book conclude with instructions for public worship. All this was meant to speak to the whole people of God. It was a call to faith and battle from God through the prophet. And as such it resounds today. What began as a problem — 'Why is everything as it is?' — ends as a war-cry. What began as a complaint ends as a confident determination to fight and to win. What began in perplexity ends in faith and certainty.

Habakkuk's problem is our problem. The answer he received is what we need to hear today. May his response to God's chastisement and instruction be our response also, that God may be glorified in the land in measure now and then gloriously, when he renews his work, when in wrath he remembers mercy.

IV. Conclusion

14.
Help for other problems

One of the difficulties which Christians face is that they have to begin to work things out afresh every time a new problem faces them. However, our study of Jonah and Habakkuk should have given us some general guidelines, some basic ideas, for treating any issue that may confront the Christian. Of course, there can be no rule of thumb; the range of problems is too great and too varied for that. Too often, the pastor's advice has taken the form, 'What you need is...', followed by his pet panacea, whether the baptism of the Spirit, or inner healing, or a course of expository preaching, or a good dose of the Puritans. (The last two will at any rate do no harm!) Nothing like that emerges from these two prophets, but we can find some matters common to both, which should help us to approach other areas with some confidence.

We must be practical

We must be conscious that we are considering the Lord's approach to people with problems, not that of Jonah or Habakkuk themselves. In each case, therefore, we see that he does not allow the prophet to be merely intellectual. Jonah is already treating the matter practically by running away. This is no mere theoretical issue for him. It affects his actions. However, even then the Lord could merely have quizzed him about his attitude and argued with him that he ought to have compassion on the Ninevites. As we have seen, he does nothing of the sort. Instead, he uses the sailors, the storm and the big fish to deal with Jonah himself. Similarly, in Habakkuk's case, he is not given an easy theoretical answer. The Lord deals with him, not just with his problem. His whole attitude is wrong, as was Jonah's.

We must never try to deal with problems in the abstract. There is a tendency to do this, especially where the question is about suffering. Most books on this subject just look at it as a problem. They attempt to justify God, to answer the objections of unbelievers — and this is correct as far as it goes — but it gives no help to the person who is actually in the middle of suffering and whose attitude may need to be dealt with before he can understand the doctrine. Job, for instance, never did receive a doctrinal answer to his problem as such. We are allowed to look behind the scenes and recognize Satan's role and subsequent defeat, but Job never learns about this. He did receive a chastening and humbling word from the Lord, which in a sense rendered the philosophical issue irrelevant. Job himself was changed before the problem was resolved without actually being answered.

We must be positive

The danger we face in looking at problems is that we allow the problem to dictate the agenda. So long as we can give some kind of answer that will end the questioning and complaining, we are content. The Lord is not like us. He never rests content with this. In each case that we have studied the Lord brings a positive point out of the question. More, he takes the prophet and makes him useful or, in Jonah's case, he will do so if the prophet learns the lesson properly. Jonah does not merely receive an explanation and a rebuke; he is recommissioned.

This is where the practical approach bears fruit. God is not at our beck and call. He does not have to answer our questions and calm our troubled heads. He is the Lord and is concerned for the fulfilling of his purposes. We may be very concerned about our (relatively) little problems. The Lord's will is that we should get on with serving him and obeying him, working out his purpose for us. How self-centred we are! Our problems, our peace of mind, our conscience and our perplexity — these are all that bother us, when we should be busy serving our God and leaving the issue of conscience to him.

This is the New Testament answer to so many difficulties.

Instead of soft words of comfort, the apostles give strong encouragement to fight the good fight. Instead of mere sympathy with our predicament, they give positive goals and definite means for reaching them. Problems of assurance are usually dealt with in the same way: obey the Lord and the assurance will come because the evidence of new life is now clear. It is not enough to silence the complaints. Like Habakkuk we must come to the point of prayer and fighting for the prosperity of God's work.

We must be God-centred

The trouble with much Christian teaching and counselling today is that it is need-centred. In one sense that is unavoidable; the 'client', the troubled soul, like our prophets, presents himself with a problem and we have to begin where he is. That is not what I am worried about. The failure arises when the satisfying of human needs becomes the real goal of our pastoral concern.

There is nothing wrong with wanting peace of mind, or joy, or assurance, for ourselves or for others. But if we aim for these first of all and above all, we shall find that we are going astray. Jay Adams deals with the situation where a man says, in effect, 'I am willing to do anything to deal with my problem.' He rebukes this idea. The man should only be willing to do what is right, what is for the glory of God. That is the only supreme end; my happiness and my peace are a blessing, a plus in a way, not the ultimate aim. We do not have to be happy; we do have to be holy. We do not have to be at peace; we do not have to understand. But God must be glorified and obeyed.

God is the King

This leads to the final point. Wherever we turn in these matters, we come up against the issue of God's sovereignty. Jonah had trouble with God's love, Habakkuk with his holiness, but the solution to each, in different ways, lay in the sovereignty of God. This is generally, if not universally, the case.

Sometimes the trouble is within us, in that we do not humbly submit to God's sovereign will. The whole idea of a 'problem' is that we are unhappy with the situation; we do not like what we are enduring, what we are seeing. So we complain. In many different ways we are saying, 'God is wrong,' as did Jonah. It is surely for this reason that Jonah had to be convinced of God's sovereignty. God alone was in control. Especially he had to realize that salvation is of the Lord — that he owed everything to God's sovereign grace. Only then was he ready to learn that God decides in other cases too who is to be saved, whether Jew or Gentile, that God decides who is to be offered mercy and forgiveness. Job also comes into this category.

Sometimes the problem is that of not understanding the sovereignty of God. Habakkuk, it seems, was not unwilling to submit. He knew about God the Lord; he trusted his covenant grace and so on. He needed to be made aware of how God rules and uses the nations of the world. He needed also to see what God is able to do with the worst of situations, in his power and for his glory.

The last word

The last word must be with God, whether it is one of teaching about the issue of sovereignty, suffering and evangelism, or the practical matters of submission, patience and obedience. God is the Lord. 'Let God be God' is the answer in the end to every problem. If only we knew the sovereignty of God properly in doctrine and experience, we would not have the problems we do. We would not always have an answer that satisfied our enquiring minds; we would not always be able to defend God's ways against the unbeliever, but we would be able to live for his glory and that is what matters. One day we shall know and understand, if not everything, at least much more. Until that day dawns, we must try to learn, determine to humble ourselves and look to God for grace to serve him even in the midst of perplexity or suffering. In all things to God be the glory.

Dear Tom ...   **John Legg**
Letters to an enquiring Christian

How does someone become a Christian?
Is God really in control of everything?
What about free will, or the problem of suffering?
Will any of those for whom Christ died go to hell?
What about those who fall away? Are they real
Christians?

In a clear and popular style 'Uncle Harry' sets out
biblical answers to these and similar questions, and their
practical implications for everyday life and witness.

ISBN 0 85234 275 6

The Footsteps of God
Christian biographies

John Legg

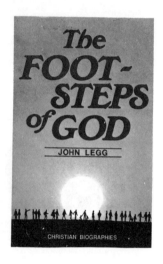

'This is how history ought to be approached: a wonder-
fully judicious combination of scholarly treatment combined with a warm and devotional perspective that
breathes the very aroma of Christ within its pages. We
recommend it very highly indeed.'

Evangelical Presbyterian

ISBN 0 85234 227 6

Help for Hurting Christians   **Derek Thomas**
Reflections on Psalms

'This book is very helpful in explaining the chosen psalms and showing what they have to say to today's Christian in our world of fear, depression, stress and sickness.'

Evangelism Today

ISBN 0 85234 284 5